Lavender, Sweet Lavender

Lavender, Sweet Lavender

Judyth A. McLeod

For Yvonne and Arthur Matthies, my parents, who never believed in less than rainbows ...and who passed on their own intense love of gardens, art, design and history

and always
for Keith

All original artwork by the author

© Judyth A. McLeod 1989

Reprinted 1991, 1993, 1995 and 1998
First published in 1989 by Kangaroo Press
an imprint of Simon & Schuster Australia
20 Barcoo Street, East Roseville NSW 2069
Printed in Singapore by Kyodo Printing Co. Pte Ltd

ISBN 0 86417 601 5

Contents

1 Lavender: The Sweetest Herb 9
2 Lavender for the Garden 14
3 Lavender in the Garden 34
4 Lavender Farms 56
5 Lavender Farming in Australia 64
6 Lavender in Perfumery 69
7 Lavender, Homely Lavender 74
8 Lavender Fragrance and Fancies 82
9 First Eat Your Lavender 101
10 Medicinal Lavender 107
11 Lavender Cries of London 114
Further Reading 118
Index 119

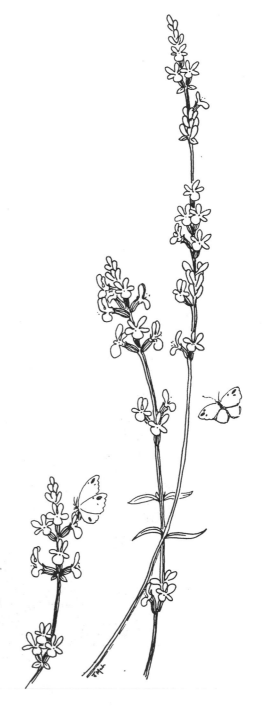

Acknowledgments

Where does one begin with a book that has been in the making for several years! My particular thanks go to Mr Henry Head of Norfolk Lavender Ltd, Mr David Christie of Jersey Lavender Ltd, Mr E.F.K. Denny, Manager of Bridestowe Estate, and to Rosemary Holmes and Edythe Anderson of Yuulong Lavender Estate all of whom more than generously responded to my needs with detailed information and photographs. To librarians in Australia and England, too numerous and over too many years to be able to list, my grateful thanks in helping me to track down so many sources. To *Your Garden* my thanks for their kind permission to publish some of the photographs supplied of Yuulong Lavender Estate. To Arthur Tucker of the USA whose information on the 'lavandin' complex was invaluable. And most of all, and always, my husband Keith whose ability to turn work out on a word processor is almost frightening in its speed and accuracy, and without whose constant help and support no books would emerge from an already tightly packed working day that includes the small hours.

English Lavender (*L. angustifolia*)
and the nineteenth century Tea
Rose 'White Duchesse de Brabant',
a perfect fragrant potpourri

1 Lavender: The Sweetest Herb

Here's flowers for you;
Hot lavender, mints, savoury, majoram;
The marigold, that goes to bed wi' the sun,
And with him rises weeping...

William Shakespeare, *The Winters Tale*

Close your eyes and sniff the scent of a lavender flower...drift into a dream of summer, a hazy glowing tapestry of flowers, a jungle thrumming with bees, alive with butterflies, sweet with sunshine...

It is all there, the heart of every perfect summer forever captured in the sweet cool refreshing scent of lavender. Of all flowers it retains its fragrance longest, only the flowers of rosemary rivalling it in this respect. It is the base of almost every pot pourri recipe.

The fragrance of lavender must surely be one of our earliest memories, endearing, nostalgic. And there is surely no plant which better instills a feeling of continuity and serenity in the garden.

For five hundred years lavender has been the quintessential cottage plant. It was never clipped as modern gardeners recommend but instead billowed into great silvery foliaged shapeless 'grandmother bushes' with a summery lavender haze of flowers of exquisite strong fragrance. They grew as much as 1.5 metres in height.

Huge bushes welcomed the visitor at the cottage gate and at the doorway, often planted together with a massive old rosemary bush with freckled pale blue flowers and refreshing resinous leaves, and a soft green bush of lemon-and-camphor fragrant lad's love. These three good friends were often dried and mixed together to make sweet bags to scent linen and act as a moth repellent. Both in England and colonial America sprigs of all three were often included in posies for visitors, or handed across the cottage gate at the end of a cosy gossip.

Washdays were made fragrant with lavender. Linen and clothing were often thrown over large lavender bushes to dry and absorb the sweet fragrance of lavender given off in the sun. You may remember that most lovable of authorities, writer of the classic fishing book *The Compleat Angler* (1653), Izaak Walton, whose advice remains as inviting today as when it was written: 'Let's go to that house for the linen looks white and smells of lavender, and I long to be in a pair of sheets that smell so'. What excellent priorities that hotel had!

The more sophisticated large houses were provided with a still room in which the mistress might produce all manner of scented products for the household as well as an array of well-tried herbal remedies for a variety of anticipated ills. From the mid-sixteenth century pot stills were employed to distil a variety of 'sweet waters' including lavender, rosemary, and sage. These were used to scent and deodorise household linen and clothing. Lavender was the most enduringly popular of all these scents, either singly or in combination. It was included in everything from furniture waxes to cosmetics.

Lavender has been loved by all ranks in all ages. Indeed lavender has ever been the royal herb of Europe. Charles VI of France (who was periodically convinced that he was made of glass) insisted on having cushions stuffed with lavender to sit on wherever he went. This might sound curious, but the usage of lavender to calm fits of madness in some forms of mental disease is at least 2000 years old and one must assume that he found relief from agony of mind in the sweet fragrance given off by the lavender.

Queen Elizabeth I of England commanded that the royal table never be without conserve of lavender, once popularly used to sprinkle on both roasted meat and fruit dishes, and is reputed to have been a great afficionado of lavender tea. This was used extensively for centuries to relieve headaches of nervous origin. Indeed it was she who issued orders to her gardeners that fresh lavender flowers should be available every day of the year should she require them. The demand of Roman emperors for the year round supply of fresh sweet violets was child's play by comparison. With all the horticultural technology of the twentieth century available, I would still shudder to obey such a command, for she intended only one species to be grown, true lavender *(Lavandula angustifolia)*. I might at least have avoided beheading if allowed to supply a variety of different lavender species, for in my garden lavenders of one kind or another are indeed in flower year round.

White lavender is an exceedingly old variety of true lavender and has been treasured in gardens for at least 400 years. Queen Henrietta Maria, the 'Cavalier Queen', was a noted garden lover and designer and caused 'great and large borders' of white lavender, rosemary and rue to be planted at the Manor at Wimbledon. All three incidentally were herbs of great magical power. She was the daughter of Henry IV of France and Marie di Medici, and the wife of the ill-fated Charles I of England. She believed greatly in the virtues of herbs in general and lavender in particular, having great stores of it laid up each summer. Many of the lavender recipes used by the queen were revealed to the world by W.M., the Queen's Cook, in a book called *The Queen's Closet Unclosed* published in 1655. 'W.M.' would have probably been an advertising copy writer in the late twentieth century. It was a salacious title indeed for a book of such profound innocence! John Parkinson dedicated that most delightful of all gardening books *Paradisi in Sole* to Queen Henrietta Maria, not only in hope of royal patronage but in genuine respect for her love and knowledge of gardens. And both Tradescant the Elder and the Younger were employed at Oatlands. John Evelyn, another famed horticultural expert of his day, recorded that Queen Henrietta Maria paid him a visit at Sayes Court when she was the Queen Mother.

Louis XIV, the Sun King, was another who loved lavender. He made a practice of carrying refreshing sprigs of lavender in his pockets and washed with lavender water.

Lavender   Eglantine   Burnet
Thyme Love-in-Idleness Violet Honeysuckle

Lavender; Eglantine Burnet, Thyme, Love-in-Idleness, Violet, Honeysuckle

Queen Victoria of England loved the fragrance of lavender and used it as a wash and deodorant. She obtained her lavender water 'direct from a lady who distills it herself', from Miss Sprules 'Purveyor of Lavender essence to the Queen' who died in 1912. Royal patronage of this ancient and beloved herb continued. Yardley and Co. Ltd of London, famous for its production of quality lavender products such as lavender water, soap, and talc powder since the early nineteenth century, are suppliers of lavender by appointment to HM Queen Elizabeth, the Queen Mother and to HRH Queen Elizabeth II of England.

Nor is sweet lavender or elf leaf or spike, to give it some of its ancient names, without its mystery and magic. It was in classical times the fragrance of the wedding night, not least perhaps because it has long recognised tranquillising properties that would have soothed a bride's, and perhaps a groom's, fears.

Spikenard, oil of spike, was used in ancient Egypt and later to anoint all sacred areas and tools of magic as part of the cleansing ritual. Oil of lavender is still used today in magic healing and purifying rituals.

Lavender as a herb has a long tradition of magical use and was one of the herbs used at the summer solstice, being thrown on fires on Midsummer Night. In modern magic it still retains its old meaning and use as a herb of purification, of love and of protection, being used in bath sachets, healing sachets and incenses. In Tuscany lavender was used to protect children from the evil eye, while in North Africa the Karbyll women used lavender to protect themselves from mistreatment by their husbands. It was said too that if you carried lavender you would see ghosts.

It has often puzzled me that Shakespeare should have spoken of 'hot lavender'. Surely of all fragrances it is the coolest. The explanation lies, I think, in the ancient classification of herbs as masculine or feminine, or alternatively hot or cold. Shakespeare would have been familiar with that tradition, and lavender was one of the herbs classified as 'hot'. Herbs which were positive and stimulating were considered hot. The ruling planet of lavender was Mercury.

And here, before we leave the subject of magical lavender, is a cautionary tale for all young ladies which derives from Carinthia:

A Carinthian Tale

Once upon a time, many years ago, a beautiful young shepherdess took her herd of cows out into a richly pastured quiet valley which lay some way above her village. Lying against a tree on soft cool grass, she thought how dull and quiet her life was. There were no young men who caught her fancy in the village. Where was she to find a husband, or was her life to be nothing more than that of a lonely shepherdess?

So deep in thought was she that she didn't even notice a young man walking toward her until he was under the shade of the tree. He was extraordinarily handsome and her heart leapt when she saw him. He asked if he might sit beside her and rest. They talked pleasantly together for quite a while. Not only was he handsome but also an excellent companion— witty, charming and interesting.

To her delight, he seemed to find her even more fascinating than she did him. It was love at first sight and he begged her to meet him again the following afternoon beneath the tree.

The young shepherdess, who was as virtuous as she was beautiful, was greatly tempted. What harm, she thought, could it do to meet out here in this peaceful valley. So she agreed to meet him the following day. He rose and reluctantly took his leave of her. As he was walking away through the forest, she looked up once more to farewell him and saw to her horror that his back was hollow, a sure sign of the Devil in human disguise!

Terrified, the young girl hastily rounded up her herd of cows and drove them to the village where she wasted no time in visiting the village priest.

The priest listened to her story and after some thought told her to meet the Devil the next day and find out in conversation which plants he feared most.

She did as she was instructed and the Devil incautiously admitted to being terribly afraid of lavender, lad's love and hairmoss. Before meeting with the Devil on the third day she picked a bouquet of these three plants and had it blessed by the priest.

Once more the young shepherdess took her herd to the valley to graze and once more the Devil came to meet her. Try as she would, she could not help but find him fascinating. But when he tried to seduce her, suddenly she came to her senses and grabbing the bouquet from its hiding place under a bush she thrust it at him. With a terrible roar of flames and smell of sulphur the Devil disappeared before her, never to return.

Since then lavender has been known as an anti-demonic plant and used to keep evil far from homes.

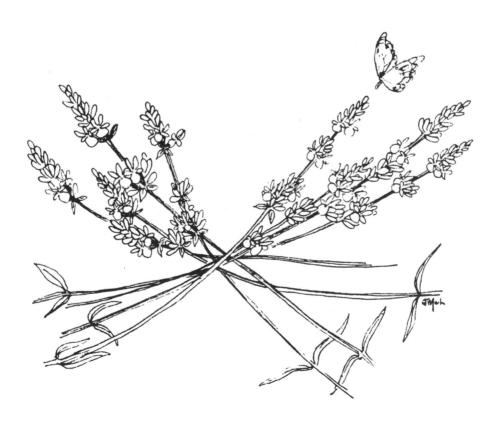

2 Lavender for the Garden

In May and June come pinks of all sorts, especially the blush pink; roses of all kinds, except the musk, which comes later; honeysuckles, strawberries, buglos, columbine, the French marigold, flos Africanas, cherry tree in fruit, ribes, figs in fruit, rasps, vine flowers, lavender in flowers, the sweet satyrian with the white flowers, herba muscaria, lilium convallium, the appletree in blossom.

Francis Bacon, *Of Gardens*

This flower is good for Bees, most comfortable for smelling except Roses; and kept dry is as strong after a year as when it was gathered. The water is comfortable.

William Lawson, *Country Housewife's Garden*, 1618

The most famous of the nose-herbs is Lavender whose flower-spike, as modest in hue as a Quaker's bonnet, is highly fragrant as well as its dusty leaves.

Louise Beebe Wilder, *The Fragrant Garden*

There are many different species of lavender, somewhat to the amazement of those who grew up with a single big 'grandmother bush', or have in mind endless fields of English lavender which they always thought of as *the* lavender. Most species are native to the lands bordering the Mediterranean but others come from islands in the Atlantic Ocean, from Asia Minor, tropical northeast Africa, and the Indian subcontinent.

Some twenty-five species were recognised by Miss D.A. Chaytor from Kew in her monograph on the genus *Lavandula* (1937) in the *Jour. Linn. Soc.* 51:153–204. All lavender species belong to the genus *Lavandula* and are in the family Labiatae along with many other favourite old herbs such as thymes, basils, savouries, rosemary, and sages. Members of the family are characterised by 'lipped' flowers and stems that are square in cross-section. Many are aromatic.

Botanically the genus *Lavandula* can be divided into five sub-generic groups. All the garden and common lavenders belong to the Stoechas and Spica groups. A number of rarer species cultivated in Australia and New Zealand belong to a third sub-generic group, the Pterostachys lavenders.

Spica Lavenders

Spica-type lavenders include *L. angustifolia, L. latifolia* and *L. lanata* as well as the numerous hybrids of *L. angustifolia* and *L. latifolia* known collectively as lavandin.

'True' or English lavender, *L. angustifolia* Mill., has also been known by the synonyms *L. officinalis* Chaix, *L. vera* DC, and *L. spica* L. (in part). It is from this lavender that the essential oil of lavender used in perfumery is distilled, and one of its synonyms, *L. officinalis*, indicates that this was the lavender specified for medical use.

L. angustifolia is a xerophyte (a plant adapted to living in a dry climate) and is a sub-shrub with a woody base, varying in height but averaging 60 cm or a little more. It is native to the western half of the Mediterranean, extending some distance inland and colonising mountainous areas to approximately 1800 metres altitude. The eighth edition of W.J. Bean's *Trees and Shrubs* Vol. II (1973) noted that it had also been naturalised in parts of central Europe, especially in the wine-growing areas.

L. angustifolia was not distinguished in the literature as a separate species until the twelfth century when it appeared in the herbal of the brilliant Abbess Hildegard (AD 1098–1180) who lived near Birgen on the Rhine. It was also recognised as a separate form by the famed Welsh physicians of the thirteenth century who knew it as Llafant.

It is probable that the Romans introduced *L. angustifolia* into England although there is no record of it surviving. It is very probable that the Benedictine monks brought it in, possibly prior to the Norman Conquest. There are certainly mediaeval references to its herbal use in Great Britain.

The leaves of *L. angustifolia* are of two kinds. The main or principal leaves are opposite or whorled, oblong–linear or lanceolate, entire, slightly revolute or plane, 2.5–4.5 cm long and approximately 5 mm wide. When young they are greyish but at maturity are predominantly green. The axillary leaves differ in being persistently greyer, more revolute and narrow and white tomentose (hairy). The flowers are lavender or purple, vary generally between 0.7 and 1.3 mm in length and are fragrant although the scent is mainly in the calyces. They are nearly sessile and ocur in six- to ten-flowered whorls forming interrupted spikes. More charming than my botanical description is 'bent outward by the weight of their spikelike inflorescence to resemble a many sprayed silver fountain'.

Individual flowers have the upper lip two-lobed while the lower lip is three-lobed. The protruding portion of the floral tube is slightly shorter than the calyx. The calyx is 13-ribbed forming a finely and usually densely tomentose lavender-green cup surrounding the flower, and is strongly fragrant as are subtending bracts and bracteoles.

Two forms in particular are distinguished in the wild, although considerable variation in height is quite common. Dauphiné lavender is markedly robust with long flowering stems to 50 cm; it is apparently less fragrant than dwarfer kinds and the leaves are at most only slightly revolute. A second clearly distinguished variation from the type is the subspecies *pyrenaica* (DC.) Guinea (syn. *L. pyrenaica* DC). In this subspecies the bracts are a marked feature, being as long as the calyx cup and broader than they are long. As its name implies it occurs in the Pyrenees.

L. angustifolia

L. lanata

L. canariensis

Munstead Lavender

A bush of
L. angustifolia,
English Lavender, in
full flower

L. dentata

L. × *allardii*

Italian Lavender

Miss Chaytor indicated her intention to follow her original monograph on the genus with a study of the 'garden lavenders', many of which are hybrids between *L. angustifolia* and *L. latifolia* which form naturally in their overlapping territories. A number of taxonomists and commercial growers maintained that many treasured field-grown and garden cultivars belong to a hybrid complex known as lavandin (*L.* × *intermedia* Emeric ex Boiseleur). Arthur Tucker (1981) of the USA and Karen Henson (1974) from Wageningen in the Netherlands have examined a large number of lavender cultivars, both separately and jointly (1985), and their work has been invaluable in identifying synonymity of cultivar names, which is a very real problem, as well as in separating true cultivars of *L. angustifolia* from named forms of lavandin. Flowering time was used as a specific character by Tucker and Hensen in keying out *L. angustifolia*, *L.* × *intermedia* and *L. latifolia* and is useful likewise to the amateur in identifying cultivars. Earliest to flower is *L. angustifolia* (mid- to late June in England), followed by *L.* × *intermedia* in mid-July and lastly *L. latifolia* (late July to mid-August).

Before listing the more commonly grown varieties and cultivars of garden lavenders, the question of varieties versus cultivars should also be mentioned. In the botanical sense, a variety (var.) is a significant true-breeding population which differs in some stable respects from the species and is yet substantially like the original species. A cultivar (cv.) is a horticulturally selected and propagated form of species which is maintained as a variant because of its appeal to man eg. aesthetic qualities, productivity, timing of flowering or fruiting etc.

English lavender cultivars can be divided into three major groups on the basis of their height ie. dwarf, semi-dwarf and tall. Not surprisingly in a plant which combines a long history of cultivation, both for its use as an essential oil source and as an ornamental in the garden, very large numbers of cultivars have been isolated and perpetuated and the descriptions that follow represent only a small number of those that have been grown.

Dwarf English Lavenders

'Munstead' (syn. 'Dwarf Munstead', 'Munstead Dwarf', 'Munstead Blue', 'Munstead Variety') A low growing semi-prostrate bush excellent for edging paths, bearing many spikes of bright deep lavender-blue flowers subtended by deep bluish-violet calyces borne on 10 cm peduncles. Leaves narrow, grey-green. Known in more than one form. It was reputedly raised by the famous landscaper Miss Gertrude Jekyll at Munstead Wood in Surrey and was introduced by Barr in 1916. A cultivar of *L. angustifolia* (according to Tucker and Hensen 1985).

'Folgate' (syn. 'Folgate Blue') A compact shrub slightly taller than 'Munstead', probably the brightest 'blue' of any variety of English lavender. Foliage grey-green, slightly quicker growing than 'Munstead' and flowering approximately 7–10 days later. Just sneaks into the dwarf category. It was introduced into Britian prior to 1933. A cultivar of *L. angustifolia* (according to Tucker and Hensen 1985).

'Nana Atropurpurea' Dwarf, compact, of the same height as 'Munstead' with silvery foliage held straight out from the stems, blossoming into a haze of deep rich violet-blue spikes, flowers purple-violet and calyces violet in colour. Sometimes mistakenly thought to be synonymous with 'Hidcote Purple' but the flower spikes are slightly shorter and less dense. A number of colours have been propagated so that it is variable. A cultivar of *L. angustifolia* (according to Tucker and Hensen 1985).

'**Dwarf White**' (syn. 'Nana Alba') A charming compact little miniature shrub rather like a baby conifer, leaves grey-green with pocket-sized white flowers with green calyces. Very choice, rare. A synonym is 'Baby White'. This sub-shrub reaches approximately 10 cm. Flowering plants may attain 25 cm. Introduced prior to 1938. A cultivar of *L. angustifolia* (according to Tucker and Hensen 1985).

'**Rosea**' (syn. 'Pink' or 'Nana Rosea') A lovely and quite rare lavender which forms a foil for the lavender-flowered forms and always evokes interest when in flower. Of upright habit with narrow green-grey leaves, flower spikes rather blunt, 2.5–4.0 cm long, flowers a delicate pink like the tender gills of a young mushroom, showing up well against the silver calyces. Tucker and Hensen (1985) considered two other pink lavenders 'Loddon Pink' and 'Jean Davis' to be identical at the time of examination of fresh material from a number of sources in Great Britain and the USA, but pointed out that separate cultivars might once have existed and since been confused or lost, which is not at all unlikely. They considered both 'Rosea' and 'Hidcote Pink' (see below) to be forms of *L. angustifolia*.

'**Hidcote Pink**' Nearly identical to 'Rosea' and differs mainly in the increased greyness of foliage and the narrower leaves. It was introduced by Major Lawrence Johnston prior to 1958 from the famous gardens of Hidcote Manor in Gloucestershire.

'**Summerland Supreme**' A fairly dwarf variety, spreading in form, with soft lilac-lavender spikes. It received the award of the Royal Horticultural Society in 1961. The bush reaches approximately 25 cm in height. Flowering plants reach to 50 cm in height.

'**Dwarf Blue**' (syn. 'Blue Dwarf') Tucker and Hensen (1985) considered the following names to be probable synonyms: 'Baby Blue', 'Nana', 'New Dwarf Blue', and 'Hardy Dwarf'. The bush reaches 35 cm and flowering plants approximately 50 cm, the flowering spikes being a dark violet colour.

'**Compacta**' (syn. 'Nana Compacta') A compact dwarf growing variety which Tucker and Hensen (1985) considered to be widely grown and distributed in the USA as 'Munstead'. The flowers are a rich deep purple and the bracts green infused with violet.

Semi-dwarf English Lavenders

'**Hidcote**' (syn. 'Hidcote Purple', 'Hidcote Variety', 'Hidcote Blue') An exceptionally good form reaching 60–75 cm in height and as much across, bearing masses of flowering stems. Spikes approximately 4 cm long, rich violet-blue, composed of violet calyces and rich purple flowers, spike compressed. Foliage silvery grey and held at right angles to the stems. Retains the rich colouring on drying. It was raised by Major Lawrence Johnston at Hidcote Manor before 1950. Considered to be a cultivar of *L. angustifolia* by Tucker and Hensen (1985).

'**Twickel Purple**' (syn. 'Twickes Purple', 'Twinkle Purple') One of the oldest varieties still grown. Leaves grey-green and comparatively wide, held almost at right angles to the stem. Excellent fragrance. Bears masses of long flower spikes. Flowers deep violet, calyces violet-green. Reaches a height of 60–70 cm with a similar or greater spread. Considered to be a cultivar of *L. angustifolia* by Tucker and Hensen (1985).

English Lavender 'Munstead'

'**Loddon Blue**' This is very close to 'Hidcote' but differs in being slightly taller and having a softer bluer colour in the spike. It was introduced through Loddon Nurseries in Berkshire prior to 1963 by Messrs Thomas Carlisle. It received a highly commended from the RHS in 1963. Deemed a cultivar of *L. angustifolia* by Tucker and Hensen (1985).

'**Bowles Early**' (syn. 'Miss Donnington', 'Miss Dunnington') This was given to the famous gardener E.A. Bowles by a Miss Dunnington (variously Miss Donnington) who bred it in Scotland. It was introduced by Mr Amos Perry of Enfield, England in 1913. It is distributed in Australia as 'Miss Donnington'.

Taller English Lavenders

White lavender *L. angustifolia* 'Alba' A marvellous plant with comparatively broad, very silvery-grey foliage, bearing spikes of pure white flowers in grey calyces. (Both this and the 'Dwarf White' lavender share superb lavender fragrance, very sweet and pure. In the 'Dwarf White', the strongest of lavender fragrance may be released by brushing the foliage alone). *L. delphinensis* was considered to be synonymous with *L. vera* var. *alba* by Lamotte, itself now synonymous with *L. angustifolia* 'Alba'. There is also a white-flowered form of lavandin which is confused with *L. angustifolia* 'Alba' and is more robust in all respects.

> ...there is a kind hereof that beareth white flowers and somewhat broader leaves, but is very rare and seene but in a few places with us, because it is more tender and will not so well endure our cold Winters.
>
> John Parkinson, *Paradisi in Sole*, 1629

The following lavender cultivars are unknown to me and I am indebted to Arthur Tucker for the brief descriptions I supply here:

L. angustifolia Miller 'Backhouse Purple' syn. 'Backhouse' introduced prior to 1962. It was awarded a Highly Commended by the RHS in 1962.

L. angustifolia Miller 'Graves' Low growing with dark aster violet corolla; calyx colour light green suffused with a dark aster violet.

L. angustifolia Miller 'Gray Lady' Introduced by Mr J.J. Grullemans, Wayside Gardens, Mentor, Ohio before 1967.

L. angustifolia Miller 'Middachten' Introduced prior to 1923 from Middachten in the Netherlands. Tucker and Hensen (1985) noted specific difficulty in rooting this cultivar.

L. angustifolia Miller 'Gwendolyn Anley' Raised by Mrs B.L. Anley, St Georges, Woking, Surrey before 1962 and introduced by Messrs G. Jackman and Sons, Surrey, England. It was awarded a Highly Commended by the RHS in 1962.

L. angustifolia Miller 'Irene Doyle', also known as 'two seasons lavender'. Introduced by Mr Thomas De Baggio, Earthworks, Arlington, Virginia in 1983. As its alternative name suggests, it reflowers each year in September, and Tucker and Hensen (1985) describe the corolla as 'dark aster violet...the calyx colour is light green'.

L. angustifolia Miller 'Mailette' was introduced by M. Pierre Grosso, Goulet, France. The corolla colour is described by Tucker and Hensen (1985) as 'dark aster violet...the calyx colour is light green...suffused with a dark aster violet'.

In Australia, *L. angustifolia* 'Bridestowe' is available, the earliest mention in the literature being catalogues of the 1950s from the now defunct Hazlewood Bros Pty Ltd of Epping, Sydney, NSW. The flowers are a medium lavender-blue in colour and exceptionally fragrant. The variety is compact and was, according to Hazlewood's catalogue, grown commercially at the Bridestowe Estate, Lilydale, Tasmania. It is still available commercially.

A second cultivar available in Australia is 'Bosisto's Variety', often written as 'Boistos', an excellent form with large heads of rich blue-lavender flowers, very fragrant. It was listed by Hazlewood Bros Pty Ltd too, and is still available commercially.

Other intriguing lavenders in the literature are 'Wilderness' (Genders, 1955), 'Carroll' (Wilson and Bell, 1967) and 'Warburton Gem' (Brownlow, 1963). The last named formed a dense rounded bush approximately 0.7 m tall and broad with grey-green leaves and delicate pale lavender pointed spikes. I do not know of this cultivar still being available commercially.

Lavandin

These are naturally occurring interspecific hybrids between the English lavender *(L. angustifolia)* and the spike lavender *(L. latifolia)*. They are cultivated in various forms and are commercially important as a source of bulk lavender oil, particularly in the south of France. Cultivars of lavandin are often listed under those of English lavender and the hybrid is not listed in a number of key horticultural texts. The accepted nomenclature for this hybrid is *L.* × *intermedia* Emeric ex Loiseleur. Among synonyms in the literature are *L.* × *burnati*, *L.* × *hortensis*, *L. spica-latifolia*, *L.* × *feraudi*, *L.* × *aurigerana*.

All the following cultivars, long in cultivation as 'English lavender', have been determined to be lavendin cultivars by Tucker and Hensen (1985). They are by no means to be despised as they are very fragrant, handsome, and excellent 'doers'.

'Grey Hedge' The foliage of this tall-growing variety is a silver-grey. The flowers are a soft hazy mauve set in silvery calyces with a lavender overwash. The spikes are characteristically thin and pointed. This was grown and distributed by The Herb Farm, Seal, Kent for many years.

'Seal' This variety originated from Hitchin where it was selected by Miss D.G. Hewer of the famed The Herb Farm, Seal, Kent, before 1955. It is exceptional for colour, productivity and excellent fragrance. Stems 30–45 cm long, up to 1200–1400 spikes per bush when mature, creating a fanlike sweep of flower stems. Leaves grey-green, flowers a delightful rich blue-mauve and lasting some four months. The bush will eventually reach approximately 0.9 m under good conditions. I strongly suspect, but may be wrong, that this variety was introduced into Australia by Mrs Elaine Hope who founded Beaufort Herbs with her husband at Cootamundra in southern NSW. I discussed some of her importations with her in 1977 after inviting her as a guest lecturer for my horticultural students, but as I did not take notes on the occasion (not at that time planning to write a book on lavender!) my memory is all I have to rely on. Certainly Beaufort Herbs were offering 'Seal' in the 1970s. It is also likely that Mrs Hope introduced 'Bowles Early' (under the name 'Miss Donnington') and possibly other cultivars as well into commerce in Australia.

'Dutch' Considered to be probably the commonest cultivar of lavandin in the Netherlands, as well as in England and the USA (Tucker and Hensen 1985). This is a singularly vigorous and excellent lavandin, particularly for garden usage, with rich deep purple corollas and light green calyces. It has broad handsome foliage with a silvery-grey colour and has been much recommended for hedging. There are a number of different clones under this title.

'Grappenhall' (syn. 'Grappenhall Variety', 'Giant Grappenhall', and 'Gigantea' according to Tucker and Hensen 1985.) This flowers late with exceptionally long full spikes of a rich purple and is very vigorous.

'Hidcote Giant' Like 'Hidcote Pink', this was grown by Major Lawrence Johnston, that eminent creator of the garden at Hidcote Manor, Gloucestershire, arguably the greatest garden creation of the century in England. It resembles 'Grappenhall' other than in colour, is rather coarse but very fragrant and vigorous. The very compressed flower head is lush, long-lasting, with rich deep lavender-purple flowers on an exceptionally long stem approximately 60 cm long. Calyx green tinged purple at the tips and densely tomentose.

'Old English' This was grown and distributed by The Herb Garden at Seal, Kent. It differed from 'Grey Hedge' in having broader greener leaves. As with 'Grey Hedge' the flowers are pointed, pale lavender and fragrant.

'Alba' This cultivar is frequently confused in nurseries with *L. angustifolia* 'Alba'. It is vigorous and healthy with slightly pinkish-white fragrant flowers, with the bracts subtending flower whorls green and broadly awl-shaped, and the calyces finely tomentose and grey-green. The leaves are significantly broader than those typical of *L. angustifolia*.

Three garden lavandin cultivars I am unfamiliar with are 'Silver Grey', selected by Eleanor Sinclair Rohde (1880–1948), author of the now rare *The Scented Garden*, 'Waltham' and one described by Bean (1973) which sounds to me a treasure. It was said to have been found growing on an allotment where once the lavender fields of Merton were situated, a great billowing plant over 150 cm tall and as wide, 'very fragrant, bearing very dense spikes with numerously-flowered cymes—an important attribute in an oil-producing variety, since the essence is mainly contained in the cymes'. It was sent to W.J. Bean by Mr H.P. Boddington, Director of Parks at Merton.

A number of commercial lavandin cultivars are in cultivation, particularly in southern France. These were assessed by Arthur Tucker (1981). They include 'Abrialii' (syn. 'Abrial' and 'Abrialis') and its tetraploid form 'Super'; also 'Grosso', 'Standard', 'Maine Epis Tete', and 'Provence'.

Spike lavender, *L. latifolia* (L.f.) Med. (syn. *L. spica* var. *latifolia* L.f.; *L. spica* L., in part; *L. spica* sensu DC., Mill. etc.), is the spike lavender of the perfume industry.

Nomenclaturally it is a bed of nails. Without wishing to confuse you unnecessarily some explanation must be volunteered for the considerable confusion which has surrounded the name of this lavender for centuries. Scientific names were first stabilised by Linnaeus (alias Carl von Linne), and in view of the huge number of plants and animals that he renamed using what has become known as the binomial system of nomenclature he made extraordinarily few errors. One, however, was the Latin name of the eglantine rose and another was lavender.

Unlike almost all botanists before and since his time, Linnaeus did not differentiate between what we now call true lavender and spike lavender and placed both together under a single scientific name *L. spica* L. (1753). In separating out the two different species later, botanists were confounded by the fact that 'spike lavender' as a term had not stabilised in common usage at the time of Linnaeus. The oil of what is now *L. latifolia* was known as *oleum spicae* so that many botanists naturally assumed that this was 'spike lavender'. An equal number of noted botanists however considered that the lavender described immediately under Linnaeus' *L. spica* deserved that name.

The result was utter confusion that has muddled many a botanist, let alone gardener, ever more. Those who plumped for *L. spica* to be the name for spike lavender then felt the need to provide a new post-Linnaean name for true lavender and, in a rash act of generosity, botanists over-endowed true lavender with three different names, *L. angustifolia* Mill., *L. officinalis* Chaix, and *L. vera* DC.

Sanity finally triumphed when an invaluable Miss M.L. Green proposed that, in accordance with the 1930 rules of botanical nomenclature, *L. spica* should be dropped as a *nomen ambiguum* (if ever there was one!). Names which are a persistent cause of confusion are specifically rejected according to the rules. As a result, spike lavender is now called *L. latifolia* (L.f.) Med. while true lavender is called *L. angustifolia* in accord with the rules of priority. There are further complications and asides that might be made about incorrect associations but I will leave sleeping dogs lie in the hope that I have clarified this taxonomic tangle for you.

L. latifolia which has also been known as Nardus Italica, lavender spike and the lesser lavender is native to the western Mediterranean region but, preferring warmer conditions than true lavender which occupies much the same area, is restricted to the lower slopes, to not more than approximately 600 metres altitude. It is the source of *oleum spicae* or *essence d'aspic* (oil of aspic) which comes principally from Spain. True *L. latifolia* is quite rare in gardens.

The plant is superficially like *L. angustifolia*, with less woodiness in the base but making a larger shrub overall, the leaves broader, the flower spike more slender and the flower stems usually branched (although true lavender can be too), and sweetly fragrant but with a marked camphoraceous scent. Unlike *L. angustifolia* the bracts have only one prominent mid-rib (as opposed to multi-veined and brown), and are green and awl-shaped. Unlike true lavender the bracteoles are always well developed.

Lavander Spike hath many stiff branches of a woody substance, growing up in the manner of a shrub, set with many long hoarie leaves, by couples for the most part, of a strong smell, and yet pleasant enogh to such as do love strong savors. The floures grow at the top of the branches, spike fashion, of a blew colour.

John Gerard, *The Herball*, 1597

The Spike or small Lavender is very like unto the former, but groweth not so high, neither is the head or spike so great and long, but shorter and smaller, and of a more purplish colour in the flower: the leaves also are a little harder, whiter, and shorter then the former, the scent also is somewhat sharper and stronger. This is not so frequent as the first, and is nourished but in some places that are warmer, where they delight in rare herbs and plants.

John Parkinson, *Paradisi in Sole*, 1629

Finally, in this sub-generic section of Spica lavenders, well worth describing is the woolly lavender.

Woolly lavender, *L. lanata*, is a very pleasing plant with broad soft leaves heavily felted with hairs which give it an almost white colouration in the foliage. The flowers, borne on long stems which often bear a pair of opposite branches, are borne in relatively compressed spikes of a good rich bright violet. Like all plants so heavily felted with hairs, it thoroughly dislikes heavy rains, looking as miserable as a white kitten that has been caught in a storm. It needs excellent drainage and a warm sunny exposure. It was introduced into England in Regency times and is well worth the effort of cultivation. It was discovered by Boissier in 1837 growing in mountainous regions of Spain, particularly on the Sierra Nevada. The fragrance is strongly camphoraceous, in fact like menthol. A superb cultivar 'Sawyers Hybrid' has recently emerged, in every way stronger than the species with silver foliage and much larger, much denser, rich violet-purple flowers.

Before leaving this sub-generic group, one variety of *L. angustifolia* mentioned by David Christie of Jersey Lavender Ltd (personal communication) sounded intensely interesting to me in all respects. It was called 'Provencal' (not to be confused with 'Provence') and was a field variety collected 'from a derelict farm over 3000 feet up in the Alpes Maritimes (possibly *L. dephinensis?*)'. It is in the reference collection on Jersey Island. Among the field lavenders in the Jersey collection are a number of selected field varieties originally bred by Norfolk Lavender and these are to be found both in their significant collection and in that on Jersey Island. These include No.9, G4, Fring A, Royal Purple, Nana 1/Imperial Gem, and Nana 2/Princess Blue.

The collection at Jersey Lavender Ltd includes the following forms of lavendin: 'Seal', 'Hidcote Giant', 'Grosso', 'Grappenhall', 'Dutch', 'Grey Hedge', and 'Alba'. Australia is noticeably lacking in lavandin cultivars (something I intend to remedy in the future as they are ideally adapted to mainland conditions and I consider them excellent garden forms, having seen them in Europe).

Stoechas Lavenders

A second sub-generic group of lavenders are Stoechas-type lavenders. This group includes *L. stoechas* var. *pedunculata*, *L. viridis*, *L. dentata* and *L. dentata* var. *candicans*.

Further taxonomic work on this sub-generic group appears to me to be indicated. Whether we are dealing with clinal variation, or stable interspecific hybrids in some cases is unclear. This has been reflected in different authors giving varietal or hybrid status to a particular form. The following taxonomic interpretations are therefore the currently accepted ones but are by no means necessarily the final word on the subject.

If the scientific classification of the genus is somewhat open to interpretation, far more so are the common names. The bitter arguments in which herb lovers may become embroiled when it comes to common names are astonishing.

Common names are just that—an everyday name used to describe a plant *in a given place and at a given time*. In England, for instance, a hedgerow plant may have only one scientific name (all it is entitled to!) but as many as fifty or more common names depending on the part of the countryside from which it is gathered. None of them is 'wrong'. If it is an everyday name used by a number of people then it is justifiably considered to be a common name.

Arguments over Italian lavender vs French lavender, Mitcham lavender vs Allardii lavender etc. may pass an amusing day but they are totally irrelevant in the taxonomic sense. If the English, Californians, Australians and New Zealanders disagree entirely over the common name of a particular lavender then so be it. If an insignificant little hedgerow plant can change

L. stoechas var. *pedunculata*

L. *multifida*

L. *stoechas*

L. *viridis*

L. × *allardii*

L. *dentata*

its name for virtually every twenty kilometres travelled in England then so too surely can a lavender viewed sixteen thousand kilometres or so apart. All that is necessary is that a significant number of people call a plant by a particular name in order to legitimise that name as one of its quite possibly large parcel of common names.

Even if some common names arose as an error of interpretation, if that error has been perpetuated and led to a significant following for that name, it becomes a legitimate common name.

What does matter however is that we make clear which lavender we are speaking of by using the scientific name. This may undergo revision with time and be listed as a synonym (syn.) but will always be traceable through monographs even centuries later.

> Stoechas grows in the Islands of Galatia over against Messalia, called ye Stoechades, from whence also it had its name, is an herb with slender twiggs, having ye haire like Tyme, but yet longer leaved, and sharp in ye taste, and somewhat bitterish, but ye decoction of it as the Hyssop is good for ye griefs in ye thorax. It is mingled also profitably with Antidots.
>
> Dioscorides, circa 60AD (trans. John Goodyer, 1655)

> Three plants...I have come to regard as the Good Companions, because they are all in flower at the same time, and they all grow happily where few other plants will thrive; the Italian Lavender (*Lavendula stoechas*), Babies' Tears (*Erigeron mucronatus*), and *Ajuga reptans*...
>
> Edna Walling, *A Gardener's Log*

> The Italian Lavender (*Lavendula stoechas*) is bursting itself with bloom splashed with the clearest mauves and purples.
>
> Edna Walling

Stoechas-type lavenders are all distinguished by a compressed spike of flowers surmounted by showy coloured bracts.

Italian lavender, *Lavendula stoechas* L. (which to confuse the issue grows plentifully in the mountains of France and particularly of Spain and Portugal), is the stickadove, steckado or cassidony of early herbal books. A group of islands off the southern coast of France near Marseilles were named the Stoechades Islands by the Romans for the lavender which grew so abundantly there. The islands are now called the Iles de Hyères. Not surprisingly, as the lavender grows equally well in Italy, France and Spain, it also commonly referred to as French lavender and Spanish lavender.

Dioscorides described it in the first century AD as growing on the coast of Gaul and it was then a popular type of lavender for toiletry purposes. The old writers seldom distinguished between different Mediterranean lavenders but *L. stoechas* was certainly one of the species employed by the Romans in their baths.

Italian lavender is early spring flowering. It is a tall upright lavender growing to one metre (1.3 metres under excellent conditions), with narrow small leaves with rolled-under edges arranged along the much branched stems. The leaves are grey-green in colour and the overall impression is of a dainty rosemary bush. The fragrance of these leaves, considerably increased by drying, is a refreshing blend of camphor and lavender with minty undertones, to some rosemary-like. The flower spikes, borne on short stems, resemble plump little square-sided pineapples surmounted by a gay top-knot of frilly indigo-purple bracts. The purple-black flowers with their minute yellow eyes are arranged in four rows rather like corn on a cob. A lesser display of flowers occurs with us in the autumn.

Italian lavender found its way into English gardens by the sixteenth century and was very popular as a pot plant for centuries. Arthur Tucker has described a white-flowered cultivar 'Alba', but I am not familiar with it. It is, however, in the Jersey Lavender Ltd collection.

Bean (1973) mentions a var. *leucantha* Gingins de Lassarez L.s. var. *albiflora* Bean, with both white bracts and white corolla. He mentioned also a plant found growing near Villefranche bearing both purple and white bracts and flowers.

> These herbs do grow wilde in Spaine, in Languedock in France, and the Islands called the Stoechades over against Massilia: we have them in our gardens and kept with great diligence, from the injurie of our colde clymate.
>
> Gerard

Pedunculata lavender, *L. stoechas* var. *pedunculata* L. (syn. *L. pedunculata* Cav.), originates in Spain and Portugal, North Africa, the Balkans and Asia Minor. Bean (1973) considered that it shows its typical form mainly in Spain in often arid and calcareous soils to around 1400 metres elevation. It is of the same general appearance as Italian lavender but differs principally in having longer flower-stalks (or peduncles) above the foliage, approximately 6–7 cm in length. The foliage is softer, distinctly greener, and the bush is lower growing and more sprawling at about 50–60 cm high. The terminal bracts are considerably lighter in colour, being reddish lilac, and more striking. The spikes after the flowers have fallen are plump and quite pale green whereas the spikes in *L. stoechas* remain smaller and are grey-green. This species does not seem to have been distinguished early. The wood cut of stickadove lavender in Gerard's *Herball* of 1633 is clearly *L. pedunculata*.

Green lavender has been variously classified as either a true species, *L. viridis* L'Herit (its current accepted status), or as a variety of *L. stoechas*, *L. stoechas* var. *viridis*. It is a native of the Pyrenees which would suggest, because of its geographical approximation to the distribution of *L. stoechas*, that it may perhaps be a variety. However this is merely speculation until the taxonomy of this group is resurveyed. This is a remarkable lavender, perennial as are all the previously described lavenders, leaves longer than that of *L. stoechas* but of the same shape and of a soft, bright green. It forms an initial upright bush to approximately one metre or more under Australian conditions, later sprawling outward from the centre. The spikes are pedunculate, pale green and of similar appearance to those of *L. stoechas* var. *pedunculata* but larger. The flowers, however, are a pale creamy colour and the terminal bracts a pale greenish-cream. The fragrance is superbly strong, a mixture of lavender and pine.

Lavandula dentata, the French lavender, is the bunching lavender of florists. It is a tall-growing perennial shrub reaching one metre in height and width. *L. dentata* has linear green leaves (approximately 35–40 mm × 7 mm), regularly and finely rounded dentate along the margins. The lavender-coloured flowers are borne on a plump compressed spike and subtended by lavender coloured bracts. The whole spike is subtended by a pair of bracts and topped by a tuft of large upright lavender coloured bracts; also it is soft and flexible unlike that of *L. stoechas*.

The more commonly grown form of French lavender in Australia is its variety *L. dentata* var. *candicans*. In general, this is very much the same as the type but the foliage is heavier and greyer and the bush is more vigorous and larger growing. *L. dentata* originated in Spain

and the Halearic Islands. The flowers have a delicious fresh lavender scent with a little camphor thrown in, but when dried the fragrance lasts only 3 to 6 months. The bush is a mass of flowers throughout winter in all but the coldest parts of Australia and is in flower almost continuously throughout the year.

Allardii or Mitcham lavender (common name in Australia) has been variously interpreted as being a variety of *L. dentata* or as a natural hybrid of *L. dentata* with *L. angustifolia*. *L. dentata* var. *allardii* is the most vigorous of all the Stoechas-type lavenders. It grows to approximately 1.3 metres in height and may attain even greater width, forming a handsome silver-grey shrub with large coarsely and irregularly toothed leaves approximately 45–50 mm long when mature and approximately 10–12 mm wide. The spikes are borne on exceptionally long peduncles to approximately 34–45 cm in length and are only loosely compressed. The flowers are a deep bright lavender-purple and the subtending bracts are a grey-green colour which makes them obscure, unlike those of *L. dentata* or the small but richly coloured bracts of *L. stoechas*. The fragrance of the spikes is close to that of English lavender but has a definite camphoraceous undertone. Mitcham lavender flowers superbly in mid-spring to autumn with us. Such is its toughness that it will grow well, if not to perfection, in the sub-tropics.

Pterostachys Lavenders

A third sub-generic group of *Lavandula* is characterised by 'winged spikes', *pterostachys* in Latin, referring to the way the flowers are borne. This group characteristically lacks fragrance or has a fragrance which is not that associated with 'true' lavender. They are however very beautiful plants worth seeking out and including in the herb garden.

Lavandula multifida (*multifida* meaning 'much divided'). This is a half-hardy perennial which may die back to ground level during winter. The leaves are green and much cut to give a fern-like appearance. The flowers are borne in thin winged spikes of rich blue and purple finely pencilled flowers set in grey calyces. The bush is erect in habit and may be in flower for six months of the year and is particularly productive in later summer. The fragrance appears to be one of those which is pleasant to some, unpleasantly aromatic to others. Most would interpret it as being somewhat like hyssop with a dash of wormwood like astringency. For those who wish to easily differentiate this from *L. canariensis*, this species is densely and finely tomentose over all vegetative parts above ground. Frost tender. Propagate *L. multifida* from seed or basal cuttings. Even for us, in a kindly climate, this lavender tends to return to a basal rosette of stems in winter. The long seed-heads twist spirally as they age and turn deep grey and brown. They repay picking and drying for winter bouquets.

Lavandula pinnata 'Jagged lavender'. The general description for this lavender is of the same kind as for *L. multifida*. The greyish-green leaves are wedge-shaped, pinnate or, in the case of the variety *buchi*, bipinnate creating a lacy appearance. The scent has been likened to that of cedar wood pencils, not an unpleasant allusion. The flowers, borne on a profusion of thin winged spikes, are blue-lavender. *L.p. buchi* is utterly splendid, particularly in a drier climate: large, dense, solid, with large substantial grey fernlike leaves. Some particularly fine specimens are to be found in the Botanic Gardens in Adelaide, South Australia where the climate suits it to perfection. I had it from Dr Brian Morley, Director of the Botanic Gardens, but alas it deserted me.

Lavandula canariensis The Canary Islands lavender is a particularly handsome plant, upright to approximately one metre or more with ferny dark green bipinnate leaves, bearing thin winged spikes of rich deep blue-lavender flowers continuously from mid-autumn to early summer and occasionally thereafter. We find it invaluable for mid-winter lavender here, although it is not over-hardy. David Christie of Jersey Lavender Ltd told me that his was killed in the hard winter of 1986–87. Introduced into Australia by Honeysuckle Cottage.

Lavandula pubescens A Pterostachys lavender with fernlike leaves with a fine felting of hairs.

Lavandula abrotanoides Lam. (meaning 'foliage like southernwood'). This species has much cut leaves, stems much branched, and is fragrant but not of lavender. It is not a species I have yet encountered.

Some lavenders newly grown in Australia are worthy of mention before we leave this chapter.

Lavandula heterophylla This is one of my more recent acquisitions and it is proving an excellent one for Australian conditions. Superficially it is reminiscent of *L.* × *allardii* but the mature leaves are mainly entire and the whole plant is smaller and greener. The flowers have a camphor-biased lavender scent again reminiscent of *L.* × *allardii*. Leaves dimorphic. Some basal mature leaves are partially or completely coarsely dentate.

Lavandula burmanii This has come to me as seed from the Royal Horticultural Society, Wisley, England and has not yet flowered for me but is rapidly forming a very well branched sub-shrub with soft green, camphoraceous entire, opposite, principal leaves, not at all or slightly revolute, axillary leaves of the same colour. I await its flowering with interest. Collecting lavenders is nothing if not addictive as Miss Edna Neugebauer memorably noted in an article entitled 'In Quest of Lavenders'. Introduced into Australia by Honeysuckle Cottage.

Other introductions to Australia include *L. luisieri*, currently being trialled at Yuulong Lavender Farm at Mt Egerton in Victoria; *L. sampaiana*, being trialled in conjunction with the Royal Melbourne Botanic Gardens; and *L. brunei*, currently being trialled at Yuulong.

3 Lavender in the Garden

The most pleasant and delectable thing for recreation belonging unto our farmes is our flower gardens...to behold faire and comely proportions, handsome and pleasant arbours and as it were closets, delightfull borders of lavender, rosemarie, boxe, and other such like; to heare the ravishing musicke of an infinite number of pretty small birdes, which continually day and night do chatter and chant their proper and naturall branch songs upon the hedges and trees of the garden; an to smell so sweet a nosegaie so neere at hand.

Charles Estienne, *Maison Rustique*, 1572

Lavender is a special plant in the garden. No other plant that I know of can so effectively create a misty cool haze on a hot summer day. The veil of lavender colour that it draws across the heat of midsummer is as refreshing and quieting to the eye as its fragrance is to our sense of smell. The soft grey foliage is the perfect foil to the flowers.

I know no better plant to instil a feeling of continuity and serenity to a garden.

Lavender hedges are, somehow, a luxury to me. There is in fact not the slightest reason why they should be. They form a delightful edging to a path framing an endpoint such as a sundial, birdbath or small formal fountain and give an ageless quality and maturity to even a young garden. For low hedging choose a variety such as 'Munstead', 'Hidcote Purple' or the rarer, exquisite pink lavender. For taller hedges choose from 'Seal' or 'Old English', for instance, or the superbly scented white lavender for something both rare and beautiful.

Mixed informal hedges or clustered plantings of various mauve and purple lavenders, pink lavender, white lavender, Italian and French lavenders, cotton lavender and silvery curry plant look marvellous together.

The earliest gardens were established for the purpose of growing food and medicine and plants for household purposes such as dye plants and perfume plants. The stability of Tudor and Elizabethan times allowed gardens to emerge from behind battlement walls. They became large places of pleasure and leisure and the homely herb garden in its formal pattern of squares

White Lavender

Pink Lavender

Green Lavender

Green Lavender and
Tea Rose 'Mrs B.R.
Cant'

Cottage plants—
Nigella and French
Lavender

Roses and lavender
flowering in
profusion

or rectangles evolved into the intricacies of the knot garden with its formal, elaborate scrolls and interwoven knots.

The patterns of knot gardens were picked out in low hedging materials such as lavender, cotton lavender, hyssop (either blue or the rare pink or white forms), taller thymes, rosemary or rue. These were kept neatly clipped. Usually various parts of the pattern were outlined by different hedging materials. The segments between were filled with coloured gravels or low carpeting herbs such as matting thymes, chamomile, savory, golden marjoram, pennyroyal and chives, or low-growing flowers such as clove pinks, pansies, primroses, double daisies, bugle, violets and marigolds.

Low dry walls can be made to form the boundaries of a herb garden. These are constructed from stone laid in informal courses to form two walls leaning slightly toward each other, the space between the stones being packed with soil. This space should be approximately 25–30 cm in width. Into the top of the wall may then be planted a hedging of lavender, hyssop, rue, silver curry plant or the silvery coral of lavender cotton.

Italian, French and Allardii lavenders, which all form tall strong bushes, are the perfect punctuation mark to the end of a low hedging.

In hotter, drier areas lavenders are the ultimate answer. Create a Mediterranean style garden—light, shade trees, and underneath lots of cool paving with big pots. Handle slopes with terracing (formal or informal), add water in the form of a pond, small formal fountain, or just a large attractive container to float welcoming flowers in each day. Fill the garden out with the fragrant restful plants of the hot Mediterranean hillsides, the soft greys and lavenders of all the different lavender species, the pine-spice evergreen rosemary, the silver-and-lavender tree germander with its 'giant rosemary' flowers, the silver of the curry bush, the subdued grey of sage, the softness of sweet and pot marjorams and oregano, and the refreshing tang of bushy thymes like lemon, Westmoreland and French.

Colour comes from lemon-flowered Jerusalem sage, or the aromatic rock roses such as the myrrh or gum cistus *Cistus ladanifer* with sticky fragrant dark green leaves and golden rayed white silky flowers like poppies picked out with rich maroon blazes at the base of each petal, *Cistus purpureus* with large silken pink flowers, *Cistus salvifolius* with sagelike leaves and others.

Culinary sage has extraordinarily pretty blue flowers. Other salvias to add quiet colour include *Salvia uliginosa* with turquoise flowers, the lavender-and-sage fragrant *S. lavandulifolia*, the pineapple sage *S. rutilans* with sprays of crimson flowers in autumn and luscious pineapple scented leaves, *S. haematodes* with wrinkled furry large leaves and lavender blue flowers borne in whorls, *S. argentea* with extraordinary woolly, silver white leaves and mauve-white flowers on tall spires, the sticky aromatic *S. glutinosa* with its pale primrose flowers, and clary sage with substantial furry leaves smelling of muscatel and black currants. Meadow sage, *S. pratensis*, has soft deep lavender flowers borne in spikes and wavy grey-green sagelike leaves.

French and Italian lavenders in particular look superb in large terracotta pots on paved areas. In tubs, the dwarf forms of English lavender are charming, particularly if combined with a low-growing rosemary such as 'Dwarf' or the sapphire-blue flowered 'Collingwood Ingram'. Prostrate rosemary and the semi-prostrate 'Munstead', together with low-growing frilly-leaved scented geraniums such as 'Nutmeg', 'Old Spice', 'Tutti Frutti', 'Apple Cider' and 'Pine', form a superb combination for a large rectangular tub.

Lavenders are one of the easiest plants to grow. Even high rainfall (we receive 140 cm average a year, sometimes as much as 200 cm on our Blue Mountains property) will not kill lavender provided it is in full sun and really well drained. Humidity is a problem though and the only three lavenders we grew with genuine success on the subtropical coast of Queensland were *L.* × *allardii*, *L. stoechas* and *L. dentata*. On the sunny northeast escarpment of the Blue Mountains we can grow them all successfully with a little attention to our soil pH which is typically acid but rich, moisture retentive, and basaltic.

Lavenders come predominantly from dolomitic mountainous areas with relatively mild climates, a generalisation, but useful for a sensible approach to their culture. From this we may learn that lavenders need excellent drainage and alkaline soil to grow well.

It is however a mistake to starve lavender. Like all plants it is responsive to a nutritional boost which is best supplied as a compost mulch applied regularly around the plant but not against the stem.

While requiring excellent drainage particularly in areas subject to winter rains, and despite being adapted to dry conditions, extreme heat or prolonged periods of drought can stress lavender plants past the point of no return. A compost mulch will reduce these effects very considerably. Lavenders are intolerant generally of heavy soils. Sharp sand and compost dug into the soil will lighten it and improve drainage, while the addition of lime or dolomite will raise the pH of acid soils to an acceptably alkaline level.

The 'true' or 'English' lavenders in particular suffer from a disease called 'shab'. It causes the death of a plant section by section leaving enough in apparently healthy condition to encourage the gardener to spare it for another season in the hope of recovery. Shab is much less common on light, well-drained soils.

L. lanata, the woolly lavender, should be particularly well cared for in respect of drainage. The felted leaf surface is an adaptation to dry conditions. The leaf hairs trap moist air against the leaf surface rather than allowing it to escape from the plant into the dry air. Grown under wet or soggy conditions this dryland modification becomes a burden to the plant, the matted fur of hairs becoming a retainer of moisture and therefore encouraging fungal rot diseases. Its silvery soft leaves make it a well worth while addition to the garden, but do give this lavender in particular a very freely draining soil and an uncrowded position where free air circulation promotes dryness of the foliage.

A trim is particularly to be recommended in the true lavenders. This serves two purposes, to prevent 'legginess', a condition of lamentable baldness of the nether regions in middle-aged to old bushes, and to prolong the life of the plant. Always cut lavender flower stalks with at least the first pair of leaves attached. This constitutes a light trimming. A relatively hard trimming, up to one third of the bush each year soon after flowering has finished, is advisable.

All species of lavender may be grown from seed, although germination tends to be erratic. Stoechas lavenders are best propagated in early autumn. At that time the plant will have numerous short side-shoots approximately 7–10 cm long. Remove these with a heel, strip the lower third of the cutting of leaves and trim the heel with a sharp blade. Insert one third of their length into damp sharp sand and the cuttings should root within two to three weeks. Grow on in separate pots during the winter for planting out in spring. Tip cuttings may also be taken and reasonably good strikes may be obtained in spring and summer although the number of suitable cuttings available are fewer.

True or English type lavenders may be propagated in autumn or early spring from cuttings taken in the same manner as for Stoechas lavenders. I take pterostachys lavender cuttings at any time that tip cuttings become available, except of course in winter when they may callous but will not root. Spring cuttings will often produce roots faster than calloused cuttings taken three months previously.

Lavender has been a part of European gardens for 2000 years or more, so that it belongs to many styles and many periods of garden design from Roman to mediaeval, Tudor and

Elizabethan, nineteenth century cottage gardens, and on into stunning free-form modern French Mediterranean gardens.

Here are some garden designs to suggest to you ways of using lavender in theme gardens that are historically accurate but easy to construct in a modern garden. Do choose a style that will be compatible with your home. Much can be done to create a feeling of authenticity by isolating a section of your garden with hedging or wooden trellising covered with fragrant climbers such as rambling roses, honeysuckle or jasmine, or with weathered brick or stone walling (if the budget will stretch to it) so that you may create a walled garden.

A Mediaeval Pleasaunce

There sprang the violete al newe,
And fresshe pervinkle riche of hewe,
And flowers yelowe, whyte and rede:
Sutch plentee grew ther never in mede
Ful gaye was all the ground and queeynt
And poudred, as men had it peynt,
With many a fresh and sondry flour
That casten up a ful good savour.

Geoffrey Chaucer, *The Romaunt of the Rose*

The period after the Norman Conquest in England was torn with civil wars and strife, and life for most was safest in association with the great landowners of the time, secular and clerical. Gardens are the product of peace and security so that in this period they were mainly to be found within the protective walls of the great religious houses and castles.

There are few remains of the gardens of those centuries that bridge the invasion of England by the Normans and the end of the bitter Wars of the Roses.

The plant materials available to the gardener in England had been greatly enriched by two succeeding waves of invaders, the Romans and the Angles, Jutes and Saxons. Among the plants left behind when the Romans quit England unregretted were sweet chestnuts, walnut, medlar, grape vines, black mulberry, fig and sweet apples. The vegetable garden had been enriched with classic Roman vegetables such as globe artichoke, asparagus, lentils of various kinds, garlic, leeks and onions, celery and cucumbers. Equally classic Italian herbs such as fennel, coriander, caraway, borage, fennel and cumin added flavour to English food.

Christianity did not arrive in England until the end of the sixth century and brought with it many advanced horticultural skills that could be practised in the safe and peaceful confines of the great nunneries and monasteries. One of our earliest records of the plants available in England in mediaeval times is the Glastonbury Herbal which was written in the tenth century in Anglo-Saxon. It was in the care of Glastonbury Abbey. The book lists both useful native plants and introduced plants including cherries, cultivated plums and pears, peaches (the Persian apple) and dates. The Herbal is evidence of sophisticated horticultural techniques including grafting of closely related species.

The Leechdom, written between AD 960 and 980, is a wonderful compilation of knowledge concerning human and veterinary medicine and herbal plants.

The English climate was milder in this period than it currently is. Certainly the Romans suceeded in growing grapes in England. The Domesday Book, a statistical record of England

A Mediaeval Pleasaunce

Key: A, English Lavender, e.g. 'Hidcote' or 'Bosisto's Variety'; B, White Lavender; C, Sweet Violet (*V. odorata*); D, *Thymus pulegium* or *T. serpyllum*; E, Garden Thyme; F, White lilies; G, Hedge of Apothecary's Rose *(R. officinalis)*; H, Eglantine Rose, e.g. 'Lord Penzance'; I, *Rosa alba* 'Semi-Plena'; J, Woodbine *(Lonicera periclymenum)*; K,L,M, Fruit Trees such as Medlar, Quince, Apple, European Plum; N, Mead planted with turf, primroses, violets, avens, Flanders poppy, English daisy, cowslips, wild strawberries, buttercups, etc.

made in 1086 by the Normans, showed an amazing forty existing vineyards. Today you can count them on one hand, all located in favourable niches in the south and in some cases grown on high vines to catch the maximum sun.

The great Norman castles were surrounded by several barriers. A ditch or moat encircled a massive outer curtain wall with turrets at regular intervals. A mound in the no-man's-land between the outer and inner walls allowed defending soldiers to see an impending attack. The inner wall provided a second line of defence. Within that defence lay the keep, several storeys high, surrounded by its own defence wall, the church, barns and other buildings.

The castle was virtually a fortified town and needed to provide a place for leisure, for quiet and contemplation, for sport and for raising food. Orchards, fish pools and useful gardens were all enclosed within the wall so that the castle's inhabitants might survive a siege. The gardens within the castle were provided with pleasant grass walks and turf seats so that one could enjoy the feel of grass, warm dry grass rather than damp, for the seat was well drained. Trellising around the garden supported roses and fragrant climbers. Trellised arbours were covered with convolvulus, honeysuckles or other climbers and provided shade, privacy and fragrance to walk beneath. Bowling greens and areas for archery and jousting provided sport. It was a simple charming fragrant garden in which the flowers were an important part. Loveliest of all was the flowery mead, a sloping grass meadow richly spangled with the gentle wildflowers of England, golden buttercups and primroses and cowslips, nodding fritillaries, crocus, bluebells, cranesbills, speedwells, tulips, anemones, Lent lilies, daisies, wild strawberries and ground orchids like ladies' tresses. The old tapestries often depicted these rich and starry meads.

James I of Scotland was imprisoned at Windsor in the 1420s and described the garden he saw each day from behind prison bars:

> Now was there made, fast by the Towris wall
> A garden fair; and in the corners set
> An arbour green, with wandis long and small
> Railed about and so with trees set
> Was the place, and Hawthorne hedges knet,
> That lyf was none walking there forebye
> That might within scare any wigh espy.

Cloister gardens associated with nunneries and monasteries were within closed walls too. The garden was basically rectangular and was divided into four large sections by two intersecting broad paths in the form of a cross. In the centre of the cross was a religious statue or perhaps a fountain or pool. Often the segments were dissected again by further paths to form basically rectangular gardens. These were raised above the level of the walk with the use of boards.

It was in these gardens that flowers were grown to decorate altars and statues on saints' feasts days. Madonna lilies brought back by the crusaders and roses, Damask, Gallica and Alba, were chief among the flowers for this purpose. In a long gone but delightful custom, monks would wear coronets of flowers on such feast days.

Within the monastery walls such practical items as orchard trees were included and the finest and newest varieties from the continent were gathered in by the monks. Pot herbs and culinary herbs for flavouring were grown in neat array and, as well, a large garden of medicinal herbs for the monastery (and the nunnery) were the mediaeval equivalent of the modern pharmacy and hospital.

Mary gardens were often made and contained flowers dedicated to or named for the Virgin Mary. One of the loveliest of all of these is the golden flowered calendula or pot marigold. Its old name was Mary's Gold.

In 1485 the civil wars fought in the name of two beautiful roses came to an end. The exquisite White Rose of York *(R. alba semi-plena)* and Red Rose of Lancaster *(R. gallica officinalis)* ceased to be symbols of war. Indeed the peace was symbolised by a third rose, the ancient Damask 'York and Lancaster' *(R. damascena versicolor)* which probably entered England with the crusaders. Each flower is parti-pink and parti-white, no two the same. It was a peace which would allow England to emerge from behind her great fortressed walls, to build houses rather than castles, and for the first time in centuries for gardens to move out beyond the walls that had restricted their size and development for so long.

Yet I suspect, in our own time, when a retreat from the world has become so desirable once again, those simple, geometrical, fragrant flower-filled walled gardens with their turf walks and fountains, arbours and herb carpeted seats, and their tapestry-like flowery meads beyond, have a potent appeal to a century surfeited with sophistication.

It is reasonable to suppose that the Romans brought lavender to England, as they certainly did many other herbs. It was far too important to their way of life, which included frequent bathing in public baths that were a central part of social life. Lavender grew well and easily in many parts of England and the absence of written records of it being grown there proves little. As well as contributing much to the pleasures of the bath it was an important medicinal herb of the period used for a wide range of problems.

But the first written evidence of its growing and being used in Great Britain lies in mediaeval texts. The Meddegon Myddfai written by the renowned Welsh physicians of Myddfai in Caermarthen in the mid-thirteenth century listed numerous uses for lavender, as did another Welsh text, Hafod c.1400. The first do-it-yourself gardening book in the English language, under the supposed pseudonym Master Jon Gardner, *A Feate of Gardening*, described 'avyndull'. The only copy to survive was written c.1440 but some evidence exists to suggest that the treatise in verse might well be of earlier origin.

The garden plan drawn here is of a Mediaeval Pleasaunce enclosed by a wall to supply privacy and hold its sweet scents within. The wall is a simple trellising in the manner of wattle fencing intertwined with sweet scented roses and honeysuckle. Within the garden, and at one end, is a hedge of sweet myrtle with an arbour and turfed seat. Lilies and Damask, Gallica and Alba roses add typical mediaeval flowers to the scene, and a small fountain plays in the centre of the courtyard garden. The orris root iris *(Iris florentina)*, lavender, gilliflowers (clove pinks), wallflowers, hyssop, sage, thyme, rosemary, violets and columbines provide colour.

The garden leads to a small flowery mead of fine turf gaily spotted with baby daffodils, true primroses, and English daisies *(Bellis perennis)*, wild strawberries, cinquefoil and chamomile in spring and early summer. Here, once upon a time, lads and lasses picked flowers upon the fine soft grass and wove garlands for each other. The true mead looked like a tapestry of rich green sprinkled with jewel-like colours.

An Elizabethan Knot Garden

Patterns of sweet herbs, fragrance trodden underfoot, a garden of simple flowers. . . this was the delight of Elizabethans. When England emerged from the Middle Ages and finally breathed the gentle airs of peace and prosperity, for most a garden was a place of sweet simplicity, built upon a square which might be viewed from windows above.

It was an easy logical shape, geometrically patterned with paths and surrounded by walkways, cool tunnels of pleached fruit trees through which it was a delight to stroll in what were reliably warm and sunny summers, if reports are to be believed. The garden surrounds often featured latticed woodwork, a charming leftover from earlier times.

Patterned gardens were everyone's delight, and as time went by the patterns became more and more intricate, outlined in clipped fragrant herbs like lavender, rosemary, sweet marjoram, box and hyssop. Grander gardens might feature an heraldic emblem picked out in knot work, but mainly the design sought to imitate the intricacies of old lace. Garden books of the time were full of advice and designs to create a knot garden and two kinds of knots evolved. 'Open knots' were filled in with coloured sands and gravels while closed knots were filled with low growing gently coloured flowers such as clove fragrant gilliflowers, wallflowers, thyme, strawberries, violets, cowslips and primroses, stock gilliflowers and others.

Elizabethans loved topiary, creating fantastic and wonderful shapes in greenery, an art passed in direct line from the Romans. There would be elegant trellising and arbours over which grew fragrant climbers: musk roses, honeysuckle and convolvulus.

These earlier English knot gardens must have been pleasant places indeed as Thomas Cavendish's poem (c.1532) testifies:

> My gardens sweet, enclosed with walles strong
> Embanked with benches to sytt and take my rest
> The Knotts so enknotted, it cannot be exprest
> With arbours and alys so plesaunt and so dulce,
> The pestylent ayers with flavors to repulse.

The tufted seats of mediaeval days were still popular, a cool and pleasant place for courting couples to pass the hours and where the lady of the house might embroider.

As the century went by the main formal garden was frequently located at the back of the house rather than at the front. The square garden might be repeated many times on larger estates to create a kind of jigsaw puzzle of squares and rectangles, all linked together, some devoted to an orchard, some to a kitchen garden, others to a flower garden or turf.

The simple knot garden was to become far grander too. The French had developed an entire philosophy of gardening around the creation of the *parterre*. In its most fantastic form it became an amazingly intricate pattern, a *parterre de broderie*, filled in with many different sands, crushed brick, gravels and black charcoal. Simplest of the parterres, perhaps predictably, was the *parterre a l'anglaise*, a pattern of clipped green hedging filled in with green turf.

Not that everyone approved of these incredible devices. Francis Bacon in his *Of Gardens* (1625) reproved the maker of such garden excesses. 'As for the making of knots or figures, with divers coloured earths that they may lie under the windows of the house on that side which the garden stands, They be but toys; you may see as good sights many times in tarts.'

The orchard was much more than a production area. As with the Victorians, and with many gardeners striving today to create their own Eden, the orchard was a place of beauty three seasons of the year, and designed for pleasure. As in all things, the Elizabethan love of pattern determined the planting and the orchard was formal in design with seats and arbours in which to rest. In spring it was for a few weeks a place of fleeting flowery beauty, in summer it was a cool green leafy retreat, and in autumn it was rich with the glowing crimson, amber, gold and jade of ripe fruit followed by autumnal coloured foliage.

Strangely, the Elizabethans were singularly suspicious of fresh fruits and laid an amazing variety of ills at their doorstep. But they were wonderfully enthusiastic and inventive about cooked fruit which was served in open and raised pies, in meat dishes, tarts, in syllabubs combined with whipped cream, in marmalades and candied.

New fruits were pouring into England as the adventurous Elizabethans explored new worlds. Figs and apricots and peaches grew beside mediaeval wardens, services and medlars and the

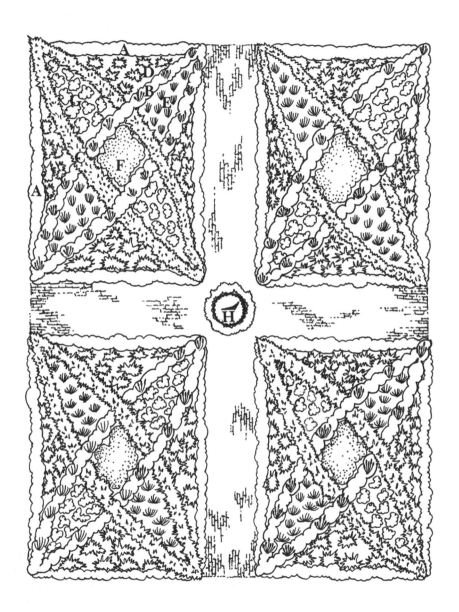

An Elizabethan Knot Garden

Key: A, Cotton Lavender, clipped; B, English Lavender, clipped; C, Rosemary, clipped; D, Clove Pinks (gilliflowers); E, Hyssop; F, White Lavender; G, Golden Variegated Thyme; H, *Thymus serpyllum*, e.g. 'Lars Hall', 'Magic Carpet'.

much improved grafted French-bred apples and pears introduced by Richard Harris, 'fruiterer to King Henry VIII'. Richard Harris, an Irishman, introduced the fruit through his orchard in Kent from where he dispersed it throughout England. Kent has, since Elizabethan times, been 'the garden of England'.

But fruit trees were only a small part of the plant riches pouring into England. Harrison's *Description of England* (1586–7) reports:

> It is a world also to see how many strange herbs, plants and annual fruits are daily brought into us from the Indies, Americas, Taprobane, Canary Isles and all parts of the world... There is not almost one noble gentleman or merchant that hath not great store of these flowers, which now also begin to wax so well acquainted with our soils that we may almost account of them as parcel of our own commodities.

Many of our loveliest garden flowers were grown by the Elizabethans. Many were yet to be developed by gaudy Victorian florist tastes and were still simple flowers of elegance, fragrance and easy of culture. Roses included eglantine and musk, Gallicas such as the 'Red Rose of Lancaster', Damasks like 'York and Lancaster' and 'Quatre Saisons' and Albas like the 'White Rose of York', 'Great Maiden's Blush' and the 'Jacobite Rose'. Then there were lilies, sweet williams, honeysuckle, violets, pansies, wallflowers, hollyhocks, columbines, the crown imperial, primroses and auriculus, lily-of-the-valley, lavender, daffodils, Mary-golds, and clove-scented pinks.

To this they added, by way of Turkey, iris such as the perfumed *I. pallida* and *I. susiana*, the lovely *Lilium chalcedonicum, Hibiscus syriaceus, Philadelphus coronarius,* anemones, hyacinths, and *Muscari moschatum*.

By way of Europe came the great masterwort (*Astrantia major*), new kinds of bearded iris, *Aster amellus*, lavender cotton (immediately commandeered for silvery clipped hedging in the knot garden), the honey-fragrant annual candytuft, and new kinds of sea hollies among others. Gooseberries and apricots were new fruits for the Elizabethan to enjoy and new vegetables included the mysterious Jerusalem artichoke.

From the new world by various means came corn, potatoes, tobacco, sunflowers, sweet peppers, yuccas, and so-called French marigolds (from Mexico!).

Double flowers, often selected from the wild, were a specialty, including double cuckoo buds, columbines, daisies, violets, love-in-the-mist, primroses and campions.

The Elizabethans loved their flowers, and knew them intimately. It was a gentleman's pleasure and delight to own gardens for leisure and for use, and gardening was one of the Elizabethans' chief occupations. How things had changed when such gentle pursuits, peppered with the scientific curiosity of the age and the cornucopia of new fruits, herbs and flowers that were pouring into England, could occupy men who had for centuries before been involved in war or at the very least in the defence of their homes. But the flower garden, particularly as the Elizabethan age progressed, was to become very much the interest of the lady of the house.

The design of mazes and parterres, the grafting of fruit trees, the planting of arbours had become a proper and almost universal subject for conversation.

Rich men found pleasure in adding all manner of astonishing features to their gardens. Mounds oddly appearing out of flat ground, unkindly likened to boils, were spiralled with a path to the top where a finer view of the garden might be obtained. Covered wooden galleries were favoured for the protection they gave from the even then notorious English weather. A bowling green and a maze might be added.

Hampton Court and Nonsuch were filled with nonsensical extravagances in the days of Henry VIII. There were endless topiary, water surprises designed to drench the unwary,

A Knot Garden surrounded by a border of sweet lavender where all paths lead to a sundial

sundials, gilded heraldic beasts glittering in the sun, a Grove of Diana, falcon perches and aviaries, marble columns, banqueting pavilions, sculptured fountains, pools, mazes and worse. The larger Elizabethan gardens could not but help perpetuate such over-the-top frippery.

The charm which we still associate with Elizabethan gardens belonged rather to the smaller manor houses and the substantial homes of prosperous farmers. Here traditions inherited from mediaeval days, that took pleasure in the simplicity and intimacy of gardens and in the plants themselves, prevailed.

Wonderful practical gardening books were emerging together with the most enchanting of herbals. Thomas Tusser (Honest Tom Tusser as he was known to country gardeners centuries after he died) wrote *A Hundred Good Points of Husbandry*, first printed in 1557. It was written in verse but was full of sound practical advice and listed 'lavender of all sorts'. In *The Country Housewife's Garden* (1617), a charming little treatise devoted entirely to the gardening needs of the country wife, both common and white lavender cultivation were described by its author William Lawson, as well as the use of lavender for hives and in the house. And who has described gardens more aptly? 'What was Paradise? but a Garden, an orchard of Trees and Herbs, full of pleasure, and nothing there but delights.' Lavender, William Lawson considered, was sufficiently comely and durable 'for the planting of squares and knots, as well as for the kitchen garden'.

From William Lawson's *The Country Housewife's Garden*, 1617

From Thomas Hill's *The Gardener's Labyrinth*, 1577

Thomas Hill, author of another early Elizabethan gardening book, *The Gardeners' Labyrinth*, was explicit in his recommendations on herbs: 'It shall be right profitable to level a bed, only for Sage, another for Isop (hyssop), the like for Tyme, another for Marjorum, a bed for Lavender...' He recommended sowing 'Sticas or Lavender gentle which is wondrous sweet both leaf and flowers' in the spring (during the moon's first quarter) and slips to be planted in Michaelmas.

The typical small Elizabethan garden shown in the design reflects the tastes of the day for a knot garden made of fragrant herbs and simple flowers, a topiary feature, a tiny ornamental orchard, and geometric gardens bordered by compatible paths and filled with the exciting new plants that poured into Elizabethan England. All is surrounded by a wall that was typically constructed of brick but might have been hedging.

In Elizabethan times lavender was thought of as a traditional lover's flower just as the red rose is today. A sprig sent between lovers signified 'true love'.

> Lavender is for lovers true which evermore refrain
> Desiring always for to have some pleasure for their pain
> > c.1584

LAVENDER IN THE GARDEN

A Victorian Cottage Garden

I have learned so much from the little cottage gardens that help to make our English waysides the prettiest in the temperate world. One can hardly go into the smallest cottage garden without learning or observing something new

Gertrude Jekyll

The tiniest garden is often the loveliest. Look at our cottage gardens, if you need to be convinced.

Vita Sackville West

The cottage garden has existed in recognisable form since the Black Death when peasant labour became a valued commodity. So many labourers had died in the plague that swept England that those peasants who were spared were offered far better conditions than before. A small plot of land attached to their cottage was now theirs to work, and proved to be an economic cushion against hard times. Here a family could raise a pig and perhaps some poultry, as well as plentiful supplies of herbs and vegetables.

Hardy and unusual field flowers such as double primroses and violets founds their way from the wild into cottagers' gardens where they were treasured. Lavender hedges, rosemary, and faithful Alba, Gallica and Damask roses such as the 'White Rose of York' and 'York and Lancaster' were hardy and much loved acquisitions. And the flood of new ornamental varieties entering England in Elizabethan times was not slow to break through the class barriers. Who would know if a slip or two were to wend its way in the evening from manor house to cottage in the pocket of a gardener?

Cottage gardens by the nineteenth century had become the working man's few square feet of paradise, and were very much the vogue too for a substantial number of an educated middle class who saw the romance and beauty of old cottages and their gardens, and valued the ordered existence and charm of village life. A similar revival in this century has seen cottages, within what could even vaguely be considered commuter distance of London, at a premium. In Australia a similar boom, linked to a rising tide of national consciousness and awakening pride in what is left of our colonial architectural inheritance after the devastation of past decades, has recently seen the same enthusiasm for old cottages. But before that, the return to the land, to old values, organic husbandry, and to old crafts saw the sixties generation buying and restoring old country cottages throughout Australia.

At their best, the gardens that surrounded cottages were characterised by an almost paradisiacal charm. Characteristically crammed to overflowing with an eclectic mixture of soft fruit and orchard trees, vegetables, herbs, and flowers, they imparted a feeling of abundance. They were plump cheerful gardens that basked like contented cats in the sun.

Cottagers have always admired toughness in plants, yet they also treasured unusual plants and were prepared to care for them. Flowers and flower breeding were popular nineteenth century hobbies proper to the pursuits of the working man at the end of the day. The cottage garden became, and remained, a treasurehouse of plants from the past. Fashion and grand ideas were not the arbiters of taste in these stable village gardens with their often conservative owners.

The design of these gardens was simple and changed little with the centuries for it was based on utilitarian needs. Ground was never wasted and, other than paths, was given over entirely to cultivation so that a humming jungle of flowers and fruit, colour and fragrance

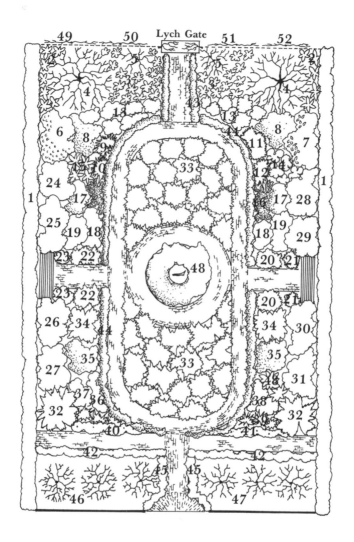

A Victorian Cottage Garden

Key: 1, Sweet Bay clipped hedge; 2, Wild Foxgloves; 3, Wild primroses and cowslips; 4, Crabapple 'Golden Hornet'; 5, *Fuchsia magellanica* 'Alba'; 6, *Philadelphus coronarius*; 7, *Buddleia davidii* 'White Bouquet'; 8, Bergamot 'Enfield Gem'; 9, Clove Pink 'Sally'; 10, Clove Pink 'Pike's Pink'; 11, Clove Pink 'Mrs Sinkins'; 12, Clove Pink 'Mrs Cullen'; 13, Violets, perennial violets and violettas; 14, Delphinium; 15, Crown Imperial Fritillary; 16, Santolina; 17, *Salvia azurea*; 18, *Campanula persicifolia*; 19, *Campanula pyramidalis*; 20, Lime-scented geranium; 21, Rosemary 'Collingwood Ingram'; 22, Fingerbowl Lemon Geranium *(P. crispum minor)*; 23, Southernwood; 24, Hybrid Musk Rose 'Buff Beauty'; 25, Hybrid Musk Rose 'Penelope'; 26, Hybrid Musk Rose 'Moonlight'; 27, Hybrid Musk Rose 'Felicia'; 28, Hybrid Musk Rose 'Autumn Delight'; 29, Hybrid Musk Rose 'Prosperity'; 30, Noisette Rose 'Autumnalis' or 'Milkmaid'; 31, Hybrid Musk Rose 'Cornelia'; 32, Lemon Verbena; 33, English Lavender *(L. angustifolia)*; 34, Costmary; 35, Bergamot 'Croftway Pink'; 36, *Stachys lanata*; 37, White Lavender; 38, Rose Campion; 39, *Iris germanica* hybrids; 40, Apple-scented Geranium; 41, Nutmeg-scented Geranium; 42, Apple Cider Geranium; 43, Lemon Thyme; 44, French Thyme; 45, English Lavender 'Munstead'; 46, Red and Black Currants; 47, English Gooseberry 'Roaring Lion'; 48, Hollyhocks; 49, Rose 'Albertine'; 50, Rose 'Alberic Barbier'; 51, Noisette Rose 'Mme. Alfred Carriere'; 52, Rose 'Constance Spry'.

overflowed from them. Nor were walls wasted. Even these housed climbing plants, while low walls became with time repositories for golden-flowered Welcome-home-husband-though-never-so-drunk *(Sedum acre)*, double snapdragons, kiss-me-quick, wallflowers, clove pinks and other colonisers of cracks in stones.

As soon as space became available in a cottage garden it was immediately filled, usually indiscriminately, with a treasured new cutting, a plant exchanged with a friend, or perhaps a clump of herbs or Brussels sprouts. Bare earth was rarely to be seen as space was at a premium and this helped to create a weed-free, sheltered, moist microclimate that many flowers appreciated. Nothing was ever wasted and compost heaps fed these splendidly rich little gardens. The extraordinary mix of plants, so different from the monocultural tendencies of other ways and days, foiled serious insect predation. And they used an excellent fungicide, a tub of washing-up water cast abroad from the doorstep. Simple soapy water is a considerable deterrent in its own right to many fungal diseases of plants.

The quintessential cottage plant through the centuries was surely lavender. It grew easily and could be exchanged and propagated as slips. Wash days were made fragrant with old lavender bushes over which linen, handkerchiefs and underclothes were dried. The flowers were harvested and used to fill sweet bags used to perfume drawers. Dried stems were burned in sick rooms to deodorise them. And lavender was an important part of the housewife's medical cabinet in days gone by, being used as an antiseptic, and to relieve headaches, aching joints and colds.

Lavender is an excellent plant for bees as William Lawson wrote in his delightful *The Country Housewife's Garden* (1617): 'This flower is good for bees, most comfortable for smelling except roses'. Indeed lavender honey from lavender farms is delicious. The frames we have obtained after lavender has been in full flower are fragrant of sweet lavender and summer sunshine. Many a cottager planted a whole hedge of lavender for the delectation of his bees, or at the very least two or three large billowing 'grandmother bushes'.

Perhaps no-one has captured these charming gardens better than nineteenth century painters like Helen Allingham, and of course writers like Flora Thompson in the classic *Lark Rise to Candleford* and Mrs Ewing in her children's story *Mary's Meadow* (1883) and her *Letters from a Little Garden* (1885).

Here is Flora Thompson's description of the most prosperous cottage garden in her village in Oxfordshire in the 1880s:

> Near the cottage were fruit trees, then the yew hedge, close and solid as a wall, which sheltered the beehives and enclosed the flower garden. Sally had such flowers, and so many of them, and nearly all of them sweet-scented! Wallflowers and tulips, lavender and sweet william, and pinks and old world roses with enchanting names...

Equally evocative is the excerpt from Mrs Ewing's writing:

> It is such little gardens which have kept for us the Blue Primroses, the highly fragrant summer roses (including Rose de Meaux and the red and copper Brier), countless beautiful varieties of Daffy-down-dillies, and all the host of sweet, various and hardy flowers which are now returning...from the village to the hall.

Cottage garden lavenders were never clipped as modern gardeners recommend. Instead they billowed into silvery foliaged shapeless bushes with a summery lavender haze of flowers and an exquisite strong fragrance. Bushes welcomed the visitor at the cottage gate, and at the doorway, together with lemon-and-camphor fragrant Lad's Love and a Rosemary with freckled pale blue flowers thrumming with bees. With their sweet clean fragrance alive with sunshine, sprigs of these were often included in little posies for visitors, and were dried to include in sweet bags to carry the fragrance of the summer garden into linen cupboards.

English lavender was the favourite lavender of cottagers both in England and in Victoria and Tasmania. There are any number of varieties, some selected for their colour, fragrance and growth habit by gardeners, others for their oil quality and quantity by commercial growers. But the original big bushes of old English lavender remained the cottagers' favourite. The whole bush is fragrant although it is the flower calyces which are actually saved for drying.

'Hidcote Purple', a selection grown at the famous English garden of Hidcote, features very plump heads of deep purple flowers of excellent fragrance. Another favourite selected and grown at an equally famous garden, Miss Jekyll's 'Munstead Wood', also bears the name of the garden from which it originated. It is also known as 'Munstead'. This is a favourite with us for its semi-prostrate habit, making it perfect to spill over pathways and over embankments. Gertrude Jekyll was largely responsible for the revival of cottage plants in her day and she mixed lavender with catmint, clove scented pinks, the exquisite pink flowers of soapwort, delphiniums and lilies, old-fashioned roses which she loved, and white tobacco.

Lavender was always mixed with other simple fragrant plants in the cottage garden— sweet williams, cottage tulips, wallflowers, clove pinks, Moss roses, old 'York and Lancaster', 'Maiden's Blush', 'Old Pink Blush', cabbage roses and others.

White lavender is exceedingly old. It has silvery white leaves and pure white flowers on tall stalks, of the finest pure clear fragrance. It is a joy to have and has been treasured in gardens for at least 400 years. Pink lavender has an exquisite old world charm. The pink is that of the gills of a tender baby mushroom and the plant is very compact and excellent for low hedging. A tiny miniature white lavender also exists, 'Dwarf White', a rare and charming creature with 'pocket size' white flowers, perfect for edging paths.

The design shown is typical of the romantic nineteenth century cottage garden treasured and sustained by an educated middle class appreciative of its pastoral beauties and innocence.

Serried rows of
English lavender
ready for harvesting
at Jersey Lavender
Ltd, St Brelade,
Jersey

Jersey Lavender
employees still
harvest in the old-
fashioned way

Bringing home the harvested lavender at Jersey Lavender

Green lavender
(right) grows in the
herb garden of
Yuulong Lavender
Farm

The lavender fields
at Yuulong seen
from the herb garden

For Those Who Would Own a Lavender Farm

For those who would like to number their lavenders in fields of thousands rather than in twos or threes in gardens, and there are many if the number of inquiries that I receive is any indication, a summary of modern cultivation techniques is included.

Perhaps the most critical points made by commercial growers worldwide who have aimed for top quality production are choice of site, selection of appropriate cultivars, weed control and control of labour costs. Harvesting and oil extraction problems are covered in the chapter 'Lavender in Perfumery'.

The true lavender, *L. angustifolia*, of the perfumery industry occurs naturally at an altitude between 1000 and 1500 metres on dry stony soils with a high pH (alkaline) in the Southern French Alps. Areas that grow lavender well correspond to the same physical parameters, ie. a freely draining soil usually on the lean side with excellent circulation of air, and a Mediterranean climate with relatively low annual rainfall and dry summers of moderate heat such as is experienced in the Maritime Alps. Excessive summer heat is detrimental to the quality of oil harvested. Alkaline soil is a bonus, but of course dressing with dolomite or lime is a relatively cheap process.

Cultivar selection is vital to success. Many nineteenth century lavender farms grew the stronger lavandin hybrids between true lavender *L. angustifolia* and *L. latifolia*, the spike lavender, which grew naturally at lower altitudes in the Southern French Alps. Lavandin hybrids are less subject to fungal disease and yield well from strong bushes, but the quality is not optimal.

Ideally trials should be carried out on seedlings raised from genuine *L. angustifolia* and selection based on quantity and quality of oil production as well as field performance in the given area. In lieu of this long term project, or parallel to it, known high quality oil producing strains should be obtained.

If the lavender is to be used for drying purposes the need for selection is less stringent, but the varieties chosen should clearly be high yielding in terms of bulk of flowers and be of intense fragrance and good bright colour.

Disease in lavender resulting in 'shab' or progressive dieback is caused by a fungal disease *Phoma lavendulae* (Brierley, 1916). It is spread via fresh wounds and sanitation is vital in areas prone to the fungus. Infected material should never be used as a source of cuttings and careless hoeing or cultivating between rows resulting in damage to roots can spread the disease through many rows or even a whole field. Infected plants must be destroyed by fire. Modern fungicides can be effective in its control but preventive measures should not be neglected, including ensuring that there is good air movement around the crop and plenty of sunlight.

Perhaps the single greatest bane of the lavender grower's existence is weed control. Harrowing tales are told by all the larger commercial farms of the time they spent getting on top of this problem. Modern selective weedicides really are a must for the extensive lavender farmer as labour costs must be controlled. Full mechanisation is only a dream for all but the largest producers, eg. Bridestowe Estate, so every possible compatible assistance offered by modern technology should be used within the budget's allowance.

4 Lavender Farms

In the nineteenth century lavender farming was largely confined to England, France and other parts of the continent.

In England the lavender which was grown both for drying and for the extraction of oil of lavender was the English lavender, *L. angustifolia*, which was introduced (or possibly reintroduced) into England in 1586. Other names for this species were *L. vera* and *L. officinalis*. It is a shrub which averages 45 cm in height with finely haired linear grey-green leaves and long spikes of lavender-blue flowers. This is the lavender that yields the true sweet pure lavender fragrance. It is native to southern Europe as well as the northern shores of Africa, and grows naturally on dry stony mountain soils up to altitudes of around 1500 metres, preferring dolamitic soils. It was farmed in Provence in the south of France as well as other parts of southern Europe.

Spike lavender *(L. latifolia)*, formerly known as *L. spica*, is also grown in quantity in southern France and other parts of the Continent. It yields oil of spike, which is more camphoraceous than oil of lavender but finds much use in less expensive lavender products such as some soaps, disinfectants and shampoos. It is also valued in the preparation of pigments for porcelain painting and varnish for artists.

Perhaps the most famous lavender farming district in England was Mitcham and its story was the story of the famous old English firm Potter and Moore. Growing plants was a love passed down from generation to generation. Henry Potter was a gardener in the early eighteenth century and John Potter who died in 1742 was a 'Physick gardener'. It was John's son Ephraim who formed a partnership with William Moore and built a distillery for extracting lavender oil on the farm which was located north of the famous inn The Swan at a place now known as Figges Marsh.

The business passed then into the hands of James Potter who was recognised as England's leading grower and was suitably rewarded by the amassing of a substantial fortune. The business was further blessed by the skill and hard work of the next to inherit, James Moore who was to become Deputy Lieutenant of the country and to enlarge the estate to 500 acres.

Such an estate must have been valuable indeed so near to London and already surrounded by evidence of urbanisation.

James Moore was recognised as a foremost authority on the growing of medicinal herbs, and the estate grew not only lavender but fragrant Damask roses, chamomile, spearmint, red roses, pennyroyal, angelica, marshmallow, liquorice, and elecampane together with wheat and plots of horehound, wormwood, wild cucumber and other wild herbs. Pasture was maintained for the horses that worked the fields.

James Moore never married but found this no impediment to the production of several children. One of these, James Bridger, was next to inherit and was destined to become a pillar of the church. On his death Potter and Moore was purchased for the first time by outside interests, W.J. Bush and Sons, at a time when the Mitcham business was slowly declining. The fate of the lavender industry in Mitcham paralleled the story of the original firm of Potter and Moore. A number of other growers were to derive substantial wealth from the fields of Mitcham in the nineteenth century, growing lavender in combination with other fragrant and medicinal herbs. Perhaps the largest of these was Messrs J. and G. Miller who owned or contracted a total of 1200 acres of herbs which were distilled in old pot-stills acquired from Potter and Moore. They were principally known for oil of peppermint but produced a large range of herbs including lavender.

The last of these Mitcham families was the Slater family who have an interesting link with Australia. Steward Slater died in 1949, his family having been in herb production for 200 years. One of the brothers, William Slater, emigrated to Australia and is known to have been a distiller there of eucalyptus oil and lavender oil.

What fragrance must have filled the air each August when harvesting and distillation of those huge crops began. When the oil content was at its peak, local women gathered in the harvest. The lavender was either bundled or placed in matting made of bass fibre for transport to the still room.

No story of lavender growing in England could be complete without mention of Miss Sprules, 'Purveyor of Lavender Essence to the Queen', who once walked with Queen Victoria through hazy blue fields of lavender. Miss Sprules died in 1912. She and her two sisters joined the family business of growing and distilling herbs, and she eventually inherited it. She grew roses, fields of snowy white daisy-flowered chamomile, black peppermint and the infinitely sweeter white peppermint. Not only did she provide much needed employment in Wallington but she was also a kind and generous employer to those who grew, harvested and distilled the fragrant produce and helped make sachets, lavender water, lavender salts and fragrant faggots.

Chambers Journal of 1894 describes the lavender farms of England and their farming techniques:

The lavender plantations of this country are chiefly situated near the towns of Carshalton, Beddington, and Cheam, in the county of Surrey. In some parts of Kent also, and near Cambridge and Hitchin, there are considerable quantities of it cultivated. At the last-named town it has been grown for at least three hundred years. The town of Mitcham, in south-east Surrey, was, for about a century, famous for its lavender fields, and the excellent quality of the oil it produced, as many as three hundred acres being cultivated at one time; but in recent years, for some reason or other, the industry has almost died out, and other districts have taken up the trade.

The plant is very easily grown. In the dryest situation, the poorest soil, and the most unpromising circumstances, it finds a congenial home, and gives, with comparatively little care, a valuable crop of its fragrant blossoms. On well-conducted lavender farms, a new plantation is formed every spring. In this way a succession of young vigorous plants is assured. The plantations are only allowed to remain four or, at most five years, being then dug up and re-formed.

When a new plantation is to be made, the land receives a shallow ploughing. Plants are then lifted from an old plantation and divided into slips with a few roots attached to them. These slips are planted in rows eighteen inches apart, the same space being left between the plants in the rows. When two years have elapsed, the plants in every alternate row, and every alternate plant in the remaining rows, are lifted and transplanted in some other field. When this work is completed, the plants are three feet apart each way, and remain in this position till their profitable productiveness has ended.

The third, fourth and fifth years of the life of a plantation are the most remunerative. During this period the plants are in the full vigour of their growth, and their leaves and flowers yield, in distillation, the maximum of essential oil. The land is kept scrupulously clean by the use of the hoe. This is about all the attention the plants get during the spring and early summer.

Early in August the flowers begin to develop, and the cutting and bunching of the spikes is commenced. At the first cutting, only those plants which are furnished with flowers nearly fully expanded are chosen. This rule is observed in the subsequent gatherings. A hook of a special shape is used in cutting the sprigs. This implement is narrower and more bent in the middle than the common reaping-hook.

When the bunches are intended for market in a green state, they are generally put up in bundles of a dozen bunches of one hundred and twenty spikes each. This is, as a rule, the most profitable way for the farmer to dispose of his crop. In favourable years, a healthy plant, three to five years old, will yield about fifty spikes. With five thousand plants on an acre, and one hundred and twenty spikes in a bunch, the yield per acre will be about two thousand bunches. The average price in Covent Garden market is five to six shillings per dozen bunches; so that the handsome return of forty pounds per acre is secured by the farmer. This is, of course, the bright side of the picture. Like all other cultivators of the soil, the lavender growers have their 'lean years'. A wet, sunless summer discourages vigorous growth in the plants, while producing conditions which encourage the growth of a fungus which sometimes destroys thousands of plants in a season.

Disease was indeed the chief cause of the fall of Mitcham's lavender industry. If the pictures created here of hundreds of flourishing fragrant acres of lavender seem idyllic, then the reality was less so. In the 1880s disease hit the Mitcham fields. It was variously attributed to the

'excessive effluvia' caused by the fragrance of the flowers, or the effects of frost, or lack of lime. Infection began to show in spring and early summer with isolated young branches wilting and dying. In time the whole plant would die though not necessarily in a season. Shab, as the disease was called, might take two seasons or more to finally kill the plant with sufficient recovery in between to raise a grower's hopes.

Then, in 1916, in the *Kew Bulletin* W.B. Brierley published a paper 'A Phoma Disease of Lavender' and the secret was out. Shab was not caused by the excessive aroma of the flowers, nor by frost or lime deficiency but by a fungus *Phoma lavendulae* which invaded the plant at any freshly cut point or injury. Propagation with infected cuttings could condemn whole new fields of lavender.

Why hadn't the disease caused havoc at the beginning of the nineteenth century? One of the reasons was that lavender was propagated then by seed rather than cutting. The resulting plant populations were all uninfected when planted out in their final position. The drawback was the variability of the material genetically. The plants differed not only in form, colour, flowering time and size, but also in oil yield and oil quality.

To standardise operations, by the mid-nineteenth century selected plants were propagated vegetatively by cuttings or less often by root division. Later plantings were often considerably closer than with the early growers, often with a cash crop grown between as is still the case with modern establishing orchards. Close planting and increased humidity permitted easy spread and rapid growth of the fungal disease. It was only later that the need to grow lavender bushes at least 1.3 metre apart with rows about 2 metres apart was appreciated. Each bush then grew to an individual mounded dome quite separate from its neighbours and increased yield per plant resulted as well as reduced incidence of disease.

Weather conditions too could affect the harvest severely. Drought in spring would delay the planting of new fields and reduce the quantity of lavender produced. Heavy frosts and freezing winters took their toll.

Mitcham was doomed too by poor selection of varieties. The finest lavender oil comes from *L. angustifolia*, a lavender which yields relatively low amounts of oil but, unlike other lavenders, is entirely free of camphor. It has a restricted habitat occurring only in a small area of the Southern French Alps at altitudes of over 1000 metres.

At low altitudes a second species, *L. latifolia*, occurs which is a much broader leafed strong growing shrub with flowers resembling those of *L. angustifolia* but yield an oil which is strongly camphoraceous. At intermediate altitudes these two species, which readily interbreed, give rise to hybrids which are characteristically stronger and larger than either parent. These extremely numerous and variable hybrids are known collectively as lavandin and they yield large quantities of oil with a high camphor content.

Unfortunately the Mitcham growers, perhaps in order to have stronger plants and fewer problems in production, concentrated on growing lavandin rather than *L. angustifolia*. Mitcham oil, although judged to be of better quality than any produced in France and able to command a much higher price than the continental oil, was not placed in the highest grades of perfume oil. When the Mitcham fields failed in the late 1880s as a result of high incidence of shab, the door to world markets was open to the French oil.

The final death knell to Mitcham as a lavender producer was the simple but inexorable expansion of London itself. Lavender growing was still carried on in places like Cheam, Carshalton, Beddington, Waddon, Wallington and Sutton and also in parts of Kent and the country near Cambridge and Hitchin. Hitchin was the site of lavender production for nearly 300 years. The physic gardens themselves were coming to an end for synthetic man-made drugs were on the way. Even lavender water was no longer profitable. For a time, single flower fragrances were to become passé. The gay nineties and twentieth century saw eau-de-cologne and more exotic complex perfumes catch the public's fancy. It is perhaps ironic a century later that the wheel has come, if not full circle for history never completely repeats itself, at least a considerable way. Interest in natural herb-based remedies is again very high and simple evocative flower fragrances have a wide following, including the fresh cool scent of lavender.

Since World War II lavender has been grown commercially in only three areas of Britain. By far the largest grower and distiller is Norfolk Lavender Ltd which grows approximately 40 ha in northwest Norfolk near the small town of Heacham. The business was initiated by Linnaeus (Linn) Chilvers, a well known Norfolk nurseryman who saw the potential for lavender growing in the area and dreamed of renewing the English lavender industry that had been virtually destroyed by disease, urbanisation and the impact of cheap imported oils.

Linn Chilvers saw all the needs of lavender being met in the fields around Heacham: low rainfall, a well drained, light, alkaline soil, and plenty of sunshine. The original plantings were made of a selection of 'Dwarf Munstead', and also 'Giant Blue', 'Old English' and 'Royal Purple' in fields cultivated by horse and plough.

Unlike so many growers in the nineteenth century, Linn Chilvers, who founded his business in the mid-1930s, saw the need to take infinite care in selecting suitable hybrids for production. Avoiding the camphoraceous strains of lavandin, he grew plants of *L. angustifolia* collected worldwide and when fully grown individually distilled the flowers of each bush so that the quality of the oil produced could be assessed. Assessment of yield is an even longer term affair, for cuttings of high quality oil yielding plants must be taken, rooted, and grown on for five years for harvesting and distillation tests. Nearly 100 such hybrids were assessed by Linn Chilvers and six strains finally passed the test for quality of oil combined with good yield. From the initial choice of a promising high quality plant to harvesting of the first acre took ten years. The consolation was to be that the foundations of Norfolk Lavender Ltd were to be sound indeed.

Norfolk Lavender's label

ﬁorfolk Lavender

The traditional fragrance grown in England

NATURAL PRODUCTS FROM LAVENDER DISTILLED

AND DRIED BY US

There was no distillery initially and the first crops were sent away to be distilled. However, in 1936 traditional copper mills were acquired from France which are still in use today. The story of oil distillation and the production of perfumed products belongs to another chapter.

Perhaps the single greatest enemy of the lavender field is weed invasion. With weeds come poor growth and poor crop sanitation. Couch grass is a major enemy with its deep wiry tough underground rhizomes. The tiniest portion left behind will grow rapidly into a new plant. Not for nothing was it also known as 'devil's bind'. Until modern herbicides with high levels of crop discrimination came in, the soil between lavender rows had to be very regularly cultivated and hand hoed for weed control.

Harvesting too was a major consumer of labour on the farm. At Norfolk Lavender a team of about forty women worked through the crop cutting it with the traditional small lavender sickle with its inner serrated edge. Like so many labour intensive farming jobs hand harvesting of lavender became uneconomical and the need for mechanical harvesting became apparent. It is less aesthetically attractive to those who watch while others work, but quick, effective and brings in large crops on time for prime quality.

For hand cutting, Norfolk Lavender had arranged its fields with rows 5 feet (1.5 m) apart with 4 feet (1.2 m) between bushes. Mechanical harvesters required the rows to be 6 feet (1.8 m) apart and the distance between shrubs in the rows was reduced to 18 inches (46 cm) so that bushes formed a continuous hedge at maturity rather than individual mounds. The changeover to the new pattern of field planting occurred at Norfolk from 1955.

The design of the initial harvester was a major challenge. Spanish workers still cut most of the Continental crops by hand and no harvester had been developed in Europe at that stage. Now Norfolk Lavender boasts its Mark III version of the lavender harvester, with diesel engines and hydraulic power. The crop left behind after harvesting has been neatly pruned for the next season's growth to a domed cross-section resembling an old-fashioned beehive. The harvest lasts over a month from July into August.

Linn Chilvers died in 1953 but the sound foundations he left have stood Norfolk Lavender Ltd in good stead since. The present director, Mr Henry Head, has done much to make Norfolk Lavender a delightful place to visit. Apart from the glorious vista of 90 acres or so of lavender in full flower under the wide Norfolk skies, there is much to see: the National Collection of lavender, a 'living dictionary' of all known named varieties, and beyond, the extensive herb garden in neat array borders the Tea Lawn opposite Miller's Cottage Tearoom where delicious cream teas, home made cakes and light lunches are provided. Beyond lies the River Itch, once used to operate the wheels of a grain mill, now drowsing in sunshine and the home of sun-speckled trout. The old-fashioned lavender-bordered rose garden leads in turn to the Conservatory Shop where lavender and herb plants can be purchased. A pretty shop selling the very extensive range of superbly scented Norfolk Lavender products is a must to visit.

The mill house, Caley Mill, is not open to the public. Originally it was a corn mill. After 1918 it was used to grind cattle cake, falling into disuse during the Great Depression. Today, carefully renovated, it is the home of Norfolk Lavender Limited, and the site of manufacture and packaging of a very extensive range of products. The present Victorian building replaced a mill recorded in the Domesday book. The Drying Barn and Distillery can be seen by guided tour.

No mention of English lavender could be complete without the name of Perk's Lavender Water, a commercial venture founded by Harry Perks, a pharmacist, in 1760. Located at Hitchin, the first crops to supply the business were planted in 1823 by his son Edward. By

1840 over 2000 gallons of Perk's Lavender Water were being produced annually. The firm continued for nearly 150 years winning numbers of international awards. It went into partnership with Charles Llewellyn in 1877 and produced many diversified products including 'Hitchin Aromatic Ginger Beer' which by all accounts was uncommonly good. Perk's Lavender Water was distinguished by a charming lithograph of a cottage called Mount Pleasant overlooking a broad expanse of lavender field.

Various smaller enterprises were begun in the twentieth century, though most fell by the wayside. Perhaps the most romantic of these was the lavender farm where lavender was grown for distillation by monks at their Abbey on Caldey Island, on the coast of Pembrokeshire. It is a picture drenched in tradition, for monks in mediaeval times grew lavender in their physick gardens for headaches, hysteria and for its antiseptic properties.

Scotland saw its own venture in Dee Lavender which was set up after World War II at Bauchory in Aberdeenshire.

The newest commercial lavender farm in Europe is Jersery Lavender Limited owned and run by David and Elizabeth Christie in the parish of St Brelade in Jersey. The lavender planting currently stretches over five fields totalling approximately two and a half hectares of lavender (six and a half acres or in the local measurement fourteen *vergées*). A total of 25 000 one year old cutting grown plants have been planted out in the fields, approximately half in 1983 and the other half in 1984.

Three varieties of *L. angustifolia* were chosen for field growing, all obtained from Norfolk Lavender Ltd who had developed these strains through extensive trialling and selection. The varieties used are No.9 (small with dark purple flowers in early July), G4 (sturdy with lavender coloured flowers in late July and good oil yield), and Fring A (a large open plant with pale lavender flowers in mid-August chosen for its excellence as dried lavender flowers).

The soil at St Brelade is very sandy indeed and was dune land sixty years ago when David Christie's parents came to farm there and enclosed it from the winds with conifer windbreaks. The pH has been raised from 6.5 to a neutral 7.0 or over into the alkaline zone with the application of lime. In addition a high potash dressing was applied (7.14.28 NPK) at a rate of 275 kg/ha to promote flowering. David has tested mulching with seaweed, traditionally known as *vraic* in Jersey.

In 1985 an oil-fired 100 kg capacity steam distillation plant was installed, made by John Dore Co. Ltd. The plants were hand harvested with scissors and sheep shears as full

Jersey Lavender's label

JERSEY LAVENDER
LIMITED

RUE DU PONT MARQUET, ST. BRELADE
TELEPHONE: 0534-42933

mechanisation is difficult to justify with the current size of the planting. Now Jersey Lavender Ltd have a wide range of delightfully fragrant, elegantly presented products which were launched an astonishing 32 months after the first planting, to coincide with the 1986 harvest or, in Jersey *argot*, the *lavandage*. At this time, when the fields colour to intense purple in mid-summer against a background of pinewoods, the sight is a traffic stopper along the Rue de Pont Marquet.

As with the traditional lavender growers of nineteenth century England, the Christies grow herbs too. An acre of culinary herbs, sixteen varieties, are marketed fresh to greengrocers, hotels and restaurants under the label Bon Bouquet Herbs. These have benefited from the local *vraic*, as has the ornamental herb garden (with its dovecote) in which approximately thirty different lavenders are grown as well as a large selection of aromatic, medicinal, culinary, and dyer's herbs. Other attractions include walking tracks through the surrounding woodland with Jersey's native red squirrels, and a gypsy caravan thought to be over 150 years old, brought to Jersey by David Christie's great aunt after her travels in England and Wales. And, as there should be, there are hives which yield wonderful lavender honey.

5 Lavender Farming in Australia

Australia's Bridestowe Estate is, like Norfolk Lavender Ltd in England, a firm which has succeeded in growing super-fine perfumery lavender and building a highly successful and enduring lavender-based business in the twentieth century.

The Bridestowe Estate plantations, named for the Devon home of the founder's wife, are near Lilydale northeast of Launceston in Tasmania. Their founder, C.K. Denny, began his career in a very different field, having qualified as a chartered accountant in London in 1911. He was appointed to act as accountant for the then largest manufacturer of toilet soap and perfumery in London, F.S. Cleaver and Sons, a firm in which the Denny family owned fifty per cent of the shares.

C.K. Denny became fascinated with the manufacturing side of the business and is reported to have become a very skilled perfumer. He began to dream of creating a new source of pure true lavender oil. Having learned so much about the trade, he realised from the start the need to develop healthy, high yielding, high quality strains of the true lavender, *L. angustifolia*, rather than using lavandin, the hybrid with *L. latifolia* which had such a grip on English lavender production.

L. angustifolia occurs naturally only at higher altitudes (above 1000 metres) in the Southern French Alps. At low altitudes *L. latifolia* (spike lavender) occurs and at intermediate altitudes hybridisation of the two species produces plants which are very variable and often very beautiful for a gardener to grow, but with a camphoraceous element in the oil contributed by the *L. latifolia* parent. Nevertheless the oil is valued more highly than that of *L. latifolia* (spike lavender) and is yielded in large quantities, so that lavandin is a significant contributor to total lavender oil production.

It was the pure form of *L. angustifolia* on which C.K. Denny wanted to found his dream and in 1921 he obtained seeds of the true *L. angustifolia* from the Southern French Alps. The Bridestowe Estate still has the original seed bag, ironically marked in fading ink for the benefit of customs officers 'Lavandula 'Fragrans'. Sample Without Value. Seeds.' That bag 'without value' was to give rise to one of the greatest lavender plantations in the world.

In that same year of 1921, F.S. Cleaver and Sons Ltd was sold to Unilever and its former general manager, resisting all enticements to stay on, pursued his dream. He and his wife together with their two sons set sail for Tasmania with its climate so nearly resembling that of the south of France. The precious lavender seed were sown at North Lilydale in 1922. The beginning of a long struggle to produce lavender oil of the highest quality had begun.

The crop produced in 1924 on a sample planting of quarter of an acre was distilled and sent to England for evaluation. Were the Dennys on the right track? The typically understated evaluation came back 'At least equal to a good French oil'. And the oil was completely free of the camphoraceous element.

The business expanded slowly, clearing the land, planting it out to lavender, building a distillery in 1930, and exporting for the first time in 1935. Just before World War II the plantation had reached 50 acres.

The war was to see both sons fighting in Europe and of course staff shortages. The farm struggled on, some of the fields left untended, and income being derived by filling the gap in the domestic market left by the cutting off of French supplies.

It was 1946 when the two Denny sons returned from the European theatre of the war and its winding down. It was time for the business to make a leap forward. The family purchased a second property near Nabowla which received its first planting in 1948.

The *L. angustifolia* seed that first came from the high alps of France produced many different colours of lavender: pink, rose, white and the entire range of blue to lavender and mauve. Similar variability was also evident too in vigour, form, longevity and in quality and quantity of oil yield. The long tedious process of line selection began in 1949 and an extraordinary 487 genotypes were carried forward to the second stage of selection for oil production characteristics. Equally extraordinary, the trials covered nearly 100 acres of planting at their peak. The final selection was made and thirteen cultivars had survived the testing, the thirteen shown to combine vigour and longevity with highest quality oil and high yield.

The Dennys went on to show that the complex of oil produced by these thirteen strains had the same fragrance profile as that of oil produced from a highly genetically complex lavender population in its native alpine region. The thirteens strains contributed sufficient complexity and reinforcement to guarantee no bias from the original oil of France.

By 1974 the Nabowla property had been completely planted over to the selected thirteen strains. It yielded a remarkable threefold increase in highest quality oil over the older North Lilydale property.

Another great benefit came from the spread of harvesting achieved. Genotypes were planted by the block so that a whole section came to maturity simultaneously. In the seedling planted fields each plant matured at different times and the harvest inevitably contained a mix of immature, mature and old flowers reducing the value of the oil. As some genotypes were early flowering, others mid or late season, it was possible as well to spread the harvesting and distillation over approximately one month.

Bridestowe Lavender Estate is immaculately run. During the harvest I failed to see a single weed between the rows, and the lavender, planted on the contour on undulating red soil, seems to go on forever, a sea of lavender blue intersecting with deep blue mountains and the wide blue skies of northern Tasmania. *L. angustifolia* is intolerant of weed competition and a solution needs to be found to keeping the fields weed free in a time of rapidly escalating labour costs. Bridestowe uses low-level herbicide applications to achieve this.

The Estate is similarly low key in the area of fertilising and pest control. All waste material from the distillation process is composted and returned to the crop. This is supplemented with a light application of fertiliser. Lavenders are anything but gross feeders. Bridestowe nominate a moth larva which attacks the growing shoots of the plants in spring as their major pest problem. Again their approach is moderate, using low toxicity, low residue sprays which they change annually to prevent resistance building up in the population. The spray is applied to the foliage before the local bird population starts nesting. By the time the new nestlings are demanding to be fed, the spray has broken down and the adult birds can safely feed the remaining grubs to their insatiable young. Although the fields are growing under dryland farming conditions (900 mm annual rainfall) the plants, as a result of such careful maintenance, have an extraordinary life in excess of twenty flowering seasons. In Europe the average is around seven years.

In 1949 Bridestowe Lavender Estate rolled forth its first mechanical lavender harvester. It was a start but improvement after improvement followed. Instead of baling the flowers a cylindrical vertical mesh cartridge was developed into which the flowers were packed as they were harvested. The cartridge, packed with flowers, could then be unloaded at the distillery for distillation with no additional handling. The current version cuts and delivers, packed and ready to distil, 2½ tonnes of flowers every hour. And that, for those who yearn for the old sickle cutting days, would require 93 lavender cutters to replace the machine and its driver! A visit in December–January just as the harvest begins is a sight never to be forgotten.

The direction of Bridestowe Lavender Estate passed into the hands of his sons in 1956, but C.K. Denny continued on to see his grand dream become a reality before he died in 1975. The present estate now comprises some 180 acres.

Apart from the oil, around 85% of which is exported overseas to the main perfumery centres of Europe and the United States, the Estate also dries between forty and fifty tonnes of fresh flowers annually. About half of this goes into the production of Bridestowe's fragrant products.

Unlike the Bridestowe Estate, Yuulong Lavender Estate is still something of a fledgling in the industry. It was begun in 1980 on forty acres of land at Mt Egerton. It was a daunting task to clear fallen stumps and tree roots, bracken, stone and huge clumps of run-away blackberries. The property is at 570 metres on red soil with beautiful views of Mt Buninyong, Warrienheip and Black Mountain from the top.

Yuulong Lavender Estate is for everyone who loves the romantic traditional image of lavender growing. The lavender bushes, planted separately in the rows to create mounding bushes as they did in the nineteenth century, stretch up the property in serried ranks. The lavender is gathered for bunching and for drying, the dried lavender being used to produce a wide variety of fragrant products.

Yuulong was established by two nurses who have worked at two jobs all the time they have been creating the lavender estate. Rosemary Holmes has finally given up permanent nursing as the farm is now too busy to have both of them away from it. They solved endless problems, often by highly original means. As Rosemary says, 'Everything we do has to be adapted for us because there is nothing on the market to purchase for lavender farms!' Even the lavender stripper was made and designed for them by one of the top obstetricians in Melbourne.

But they are achieving a great deal. Television, radio and magazines have all spread the word about Yuulong Lavender Estate. The first year they opened to visitors 2000 people came for the open weekend. Last season 5000 came. The charm of Yuulong is becoming known.

Yuulong have built up a reference collection of lavenders and now have nineteen species and varieties for visitors to see, together with old-fashioned perennial gardens. And if you have never seen lavender harvested the old-fashioned way with a sickle, this is the place to see it.

In the craft shop on the Estate is a fragrant array of lavender crafts, from lavender massage oil, bath oil, bath salts, lavender soap, and lavender umbrellas to teazel ladies. There is also dried lavender, pot pourri, lavender mustard, lavender biscuits and all manner of other fragrant treats. The special Open Weekend marks the beginning of the lavender season around the second weekend in December, then carries on to the end of February. After that the Lavender Estate is closed to the public.

A little known piece of Australian history is the story of the Lavender Lady. I have copies of two books written by the Lavender Lady, Evaline Ferguson, who grew a small sea of cutting lavender in Lindfield, Sydney in the 1930s. It is difficult to believe such a garden existed in Lindfield nearly sixty years ago. The old photograph I have from the *Sydney Morning Herald* might have been taken in the Scilly Isles with a smartly dressed lady in a large shady hat picking French lavender *(L. dentata)* flowers, in the background a villa, palms, eucalyptus and pines behind tall clipped hedges. It is enough to make anyone wish that Sydney might

The miniature lavender farm of the 'Lavender Lady', Evaline Ferguson, at 'Eurella', Lindfield, in the mid-1930s. Photograph supplied by Margaret Ferguson.

have had the good sense to stop growing and choking in its own pollution. But then the same can be said of London which laid down bitumen and bricks and concrete over fertile land that had grown countless acres of lavender and sweet herbs and roses.

The Lavender Lady's fragrant patch began with one large old bush of French lavender that grew along the side of her home. French lavender grows very well indeed in Sydney but the Lavender Lady considered herself no gardener and was much surprised when a batch of cuttings took, grew sturdy and bloomed beautifully. Time after time she revisited what she had come to regard as her 'grandmother's bush' for cuttings until a very large suburban garden had turned into a misty sea of lavender, a Miniature Farm as she called it.

Indeed the *Sydney Morning Herald* carried an article 'The Lavender Lady. How one bush grew into a farm.' The article caused an unbelievable amount of interest. Letters poured in, not only from Australia but from overseas as many clippings were sent abroad. Visitors poured in some of them travelling hundreds of miles to see the lavender. Such was the power of lavender to attract, then and now.

The lavender, which was beautifully bunched in posies, was sold as 'Quality Street Lavender'. It was greatly in demand for almost every occasion. She grew English lavender in small amounts too but it was for bunching lavender that she was known. Her two little books *Lavender Lovers* and *Lavender Levels* are now rare treasures and a reminder of a very different Sydney.

Lavenders are a feature of Honeysuckle Cottage at Bowen Mountain on the northeast side of the Blue Mountains in New South Wales, a nursery listing approximately 2000 pre-twentieth century ornamental cultivars with several acres of old country gardens planted with roses, herbs, perennials, fragrant shrubs and trees of past centuries. The nursery houses a reference collection of lavender species and varieties and there are extensive plantings and lavender walks within the gardens. Fragrant lavender gifts are a feature of The Stillroom, the gift shop associated with the nursery. A reference collection for Victoria is housed at Yuulong Lavender Estate.

The cover illustration from *Lavender Levels* by the 'Lavender Lady'

6 Lavender in Perfumery

The production of lavender for distillation is an important branch of the industry. In the country of Surrey there are several large lavender distilleries. To these the growers carry their harvestings to be subjected to the necessary process. The oil is contained in glands situated chiefly on the calyx, corolla, and leaves, but also to a less extent on the branches and flower-stalks. In the process of distillation, two hours are allowed for the first 'run'. This run gives the clearest and best oil; and when of a very high quality, it is almost colourless. For the second run four hours are allowed, the oil produced being of a pale amber tint, and having a stronger, coarser odour than that which results from the first run. When the highest quality of oil is desired, flowers only are used in the process. The quality of the oil secured depends also on the kind of season in which the flowers have been grown. Sunless summers result in a much reduced quantity and inferior quality. There are many acres of land throughout the kingdom, producing at present only a scanty crop of grass, which might be used for the cultivation of the lavender plant. The demand for it is practically unlimited, and there is therefore little danger of it being produced in such quantities that the price would fall below a remunerative level.

Chambers Journal, 1894

Extracting the essential oils of plants to obtain a product of the highest quality is a delicate art as well as a science. Many flowers have essential oils which are unstable and they are extracted by the ancient art of *enfleurage*. The process consists in transferring the volatile oil to a thin layer of carrier grease at room temperature to form an initial 'pomade' for further extraction. Flowers must retain their fragrance for between twelve and twenty-four hours after cutting, and justify the expense of so much hand labour. Flowers still extracted by this process include jonquils, jasmine, orange blossom, tuberoses, freesias, daphne and carnations. The final product, 'floral absolute', is a concentrated mixture of essential oils and is often literally worth its weight in gold or considerably more.

A second type of essential oil extraction is by maceration, a process in which floral, fruit or leaf material is steeped in oil at room temperature or, depending on the material involved, in hot oil. Rose petals, for instance, are extracted by cool temperature maceration. Commercially, the petals are usually removed at the end of 48 hours and the oil charged with a new volume of petals.

A third type of essential oil extraction is by expression, the oil being mechanically released from ruptured oil glands. Oil of bergamot from *Citrus aurantium* var. *bergania*, oil of pettigrain from the wild orange *(Citrus vulgaris)* and oil of orange from the sweet orange *(Citrus aurantium* var. *sinsensi)* are examples of essential oils extracted in this way.

Essential oil of lavender is somewhat unusual among the perfumery oils in being sufficiently stable to withstand the process of steam distillation. The essential oil is contained principally in microscopic glands in the calyx and to some degree in the lip of the corolla.

The art of distillation is an ancient one. But it was little practised in England until the sixteenth century. Hieronymous Brunschling's benchmark two volume book on distillation *Liber De Arte Distillandi* (1500 and 1507, Strasbourg) was issued in an age when distillation became popular not only with the medical fraternity to which Brunschling belonged but also with housewives, for by the middle of the sixteenth century the making of innumerable sweet waters in the stillrooms of large houses was common. Rosemary, lavender, balm, tansy and sage were all popular subjects for the technique.

Until the beginning of the twentieth century, the universal process involved water distillation. The flowers were placed in a water bath connected to a condenser. The water was heated to boiling point by fire and the oil inside the plant material volatalised and passed through the condenser together with the steam. The two layers of cooled oil and water quickly separated out in the collecting vessel, the upper layer being the essential oil. Portable pot stills of this kind were used to distil harvests of wild lavender *in situ* in France and large stills of this kind were used in Mitcham and surrounding lavender producing areas in England. Distillation time for lavender in Mitcham for the first run was four hours and yielded the best quality, almost colourless oil. The second run of two hours yielded a second grade yellowish oil with a camphoraceous coarser odour. Other herbs distilled in this way included rosemary, sage, geranium and peppermint.

Immersion in water however is an unnecessary step and the more rapid steam distillation technique superseded water distillation in England. This is the technique now used, for instance, at Norfolk Lavender Ltd and Jersey Lavender Ltd and at Bridestowe Estate in Tasmania. Steam is passed through harvested flowers which have been packed down in the distillation chamber. Treading down the herbs was an aromatic if now mainly extinct profession. In most cases flowers and stalks were distilled, as they are today, but sometimes the flowers were stripped from the stalks before distillation, which made the process highly labour intensive.

A further sophistication introduced in 1957 at Bridestowe Estate in Tasmania led to an innovative modification of the mechanical harvester so that cartridge-style liners are filled

Field cut English
lavender being
lowered into the
steam distillation unit
at Jersey Lavender
Ltd

Pale golden lavender
oil at the completion
of a distillation run
at Jersey Lavender

David Christie
assessing the quality
of lavender oil being
distilled from his
crop at St Brelade,
Jersey

The start of harveting in January at Bridestowe Estate, Lilydale, Tasmania. The harvester packs lavender directly into a cartridge for distilling

The high speed stills seen from the mezzanine level at Bridestowe Estate

The separator bench in the large distillery at the Bridestowe Estate

directly in the field with the harvested lavender. The filled cartridge liners are then transported to the distillery and placed directly into the distilling vats. Each cartridge has a quarter ton capacity and a wire mesh base.

The resulting oil needs to be set aside for some time to mature as it is a very complex mixture and has a raw odour immediately after distillation. For the first twenty-four hours it is stored with a dessicant to remove any remaining free water. It can be used after four months maturation, but like fine wine continues to improve in the barrel for several years.

It is worth noting incidentally that Bridestowe's distillation process used to take 75 minutes and is now down to 17 minutes, with a corresponding increase in yield. A vast improvement on the four to six hours characteristic of the nineteenth century! Bridestowe Estate maintain a standard bulking mixture of the genotypes in the field each year in order to guarantee consistency of fragrance in their product, and store the oil in special tin-lined drums under inert gas to prevent any oxidation occurring.

Oil of spike emanates mainly from Spain and is distilled from *L. latifolia*. A large volume of oil derived from lavandin, a hybrid complex derived from *L. angustifolia* and L. latifolia, is produced annually, largely from France. It lacks the purity of true oil of lavender from *L. angustifolia*, having a camphoraceous element, but is very popular in perfuming less expensive toiletry articles such as soap.

True lavender oil, on the other hand, finds many uses in the perfumery business. It is used in the making of lavender toilet water, lavender perfumes and colognes, but this is far from the end of the story.

Lavender's fortunes in many ways parallel those of society. Perfume was largely the province of the affluent in previous centuries because it depended upon natural flower essential oils. As the demand for perfumes increased, due to the needs of a growing and increasingly affluent middle class, the ability of the essential oil suppliers to respond to the demand was stretched to the limit. However, an increasingly sophisticated pharmaceutical industry was beginning to manufacture and supply a number of synthetic aromatics.

Synthetic aromatics are 'single note' materials with no subtlety. In general, a perfume based on synthetics alone would generally be singularly harsh and 'cheap'. Essential oils extracted from nature are very complex mixtures in their own right. Their very complexity allows for subtlety of fragrance, for soft blendings rather than harsh 'edges' in the final perfume product.

Lavender oil derived from true lavender was an ideal blending oil providing a subtle and very complex mixture of volatiles that helped to smooth out fragrances made in part or whole from synthetic aromatics. The demand for it spiralled from World War I onward and today it is a very important raw material in a large number of perfumes.

7 Lavender, Homely Lavender

An honest ale-house where we shall find a cleanly room, lavender in the windows, and twenty ballads struck about the wall.

Piscator, in Izaak Walton's The Compleat Angler, 1653

Good master, let's go to that house, for the linen looks white and smells of lavender, and I long to lie in a pair of sheets that smell so.

Izaak Walton, 1682

Boil it in water, wet they shirt in it, dry it again and wear it . . .

William Langham

Lavender, honest, well-loved, long-lived, most gentle and evocative of all fragrances has found its way into so many aspects of homelife. The very name 'lavender' is supposedly derived from the Latin *lavare* meaning 'to wash', for the Romans used it extensively as a bath perfume, throwing bundles of lavender into their baths. The lavender used might have been what we now call English lavender but could also have been *Lavandula dentata, Lavandula latifolia* or *Lavandula stoechas*, for all were much used.

Since that time, with the greatest ingenuity, ladies in particular have found many ways to delight their households with the fragrance of lavender. And lavender has long been a symbol for cleanliness and purity. Today we know that lavender has antiseptic properties and was most properly associated with an orderly household, for it is both a strong and beautifully scented domestic disinfectant.

How delightful a scene Izaak Walton evoked in that most gentle and gentlemanly of all books, *The Compleat Angler* (1653), when he described his honest ale-house with pots of lavender in the windows. It was the custom once, and surely should again be so, to place pots of sweet flowering lavender and refreshing rosemary on sunny windowsills to perfume the air.

John Parkinson, writer of perhaps the most delightful of all gardening books, *Paradisi in Sole, Paradisus Terrestris, or, A Garden of Pleasant Flowers* (1629), loved lavender and wrote of how its fragrance on a handkerchief would pierce the senses in a most refreshing manner. Many, many generations later, it still does. Many a child now grown up will remember having a little lavender water dabbed on a handkerchief to be surreptitiously sniffed throughout the more boring parts of the day, or lavender water applied to feverish and aching brows.

In that wonderfully entertaining nineteenth century novel *Cranford*, centred around a village of 'Amazons', Mrs Gaskell spoke of 'little bunches of lavender flowers sent to strew the drawers of some town dweller, or to burn in the room of some invalid'.

The Victorians were excessively fond of lavender and used lavender furniture wax, washed their floors with lavender water, hung the backs of armchairs with lavender bags, and had their linen and clothing 'laid up in lavender'. Indeed lavender was a well-known moth repellent often combined with another moth repellent herb, lemon-and-camphor scented lad's love. So it was a practical as well as a fragrant practice.

Yet these practices were already centuries old, a part of Elizabethan life long before the Victorians adopted them with such enthusiasm. Indeed one speculates whether having a reigning queen of England has not prompted a return to housewifely virtues and the gentle art of herb growing. The reigns of Queen Elizabeth I, Queen Victoria, and our present Queen Elizabeth II have all seen a resurgence in interest in herbs and their use in the home and garden. All three reigns have been characterised by stability in otherwise difficult times and by emphasis on the simple virtues and lasting values of life.

I can just remember the days when cotton sheets were always bleached to purest white by fresh clean air, breezes and brilliant sun, then ironed and laid up in lavender. And no dreams were sweeter than those that came on crisp white lavender-scented sheets and pillows. Alas, no matter how pretty the printed sheets and pillowslips in cotton and terylene mix that we have thirty years later, they do not smell of sunshine and lavender as they once did. So these days I confess to sprinkling the pillowslips lightly with lavender water at night. And even on the hottest nights when one might otherwise be fretting and tossing, the cool sleep-inducing scent of lavender works magic.

It was an old tradition to plant a hedge of lavender near the laundry door. On sunny days handkerchiefs, pillowslips and lacy camisoles and petticoats might be seen drying decorously away from prying eyes in the warmth of the sun. How much more pleasant to have lavender wash days than tumble driers!

When time permits I still delight in spreading as many items of washing as possible, including pillow cases, to dry over our huge old bushes of French and Allardii lavender, and over hedges of English lavender. The sun's warmth extracts the sweet fragrant oil of lavender into the air to permeate the drying washing. Almost the same effect can be achieved by storing sheets fresh from the sun and wind with lavender bags between each folded sheet.

Drawer pillows are a pretty conceit that were once widely used to perfume stored linens. These were made with thin porous fabric, approximately 15 cm long and 10 cm wide, quilted and beribboned. They were filled with various deliciously fragrant mixtures of dried herbs and petals. Some classic old mixtures included: lavender, rose petals, sweet marjoram and rose geranium; rose geranium leaves and sweet verbena leaves; costmary with rose geranium leaves.

Sweet sachets were another pretty and fragrant idea and consisted of little taffeta, organdie or silk bags frilled with lace and filled with fragrant mixtures. The sachets were tied up with satin ribbons and hung in wardrobes or placed in drawers. Here are some traditional fragrant sachet mixes:

- Lavender, rose geranium leaves, roses, lemon verbena
- Lavender, rosemary, a few cloves, dried crushed zest of oranges and lemons, orange scented geranium
- Mixed scented geraniums and rosemary
- Peppermint, lemon verbena, rose geranium, lavender, rose petals, peppermint geranium
- Lemon thyme, lemon verbena, lemon-scented tea-tree, lavender.
- Costmary, lemon-scented geranium leaves

Lavender cosmetic vinegar was once a favourite. A few drops were added to the final rinse after a shampoo to remove the film of soap left behind and to clear the scalp of flaky old soap residue. Its antiseptic qualities and acid pH would have been helpful in maintaining the health of the scalp. It made a refreshing scent to dab behind the ears and on the forehead.

Lavender cosmetic vinegar can still be purchased but it can cost a great deal. Yet it is relatively easy and inexpensive to make. Here is the traditional recipe:

Lavender Cosmetic Vinegar

White wine vinegar
Freshly gathered heads of lavender with the dew dried from them

Fill a glass jar with whole heads of lavender blossoms, and cover with white wine vinegar. Leave the jar with a plastic lid on in a sunny place for 2 weeks, shaking the bottle each day.

Empty the bottle, straining out the vinegar. Refill the bottle with fresh lavender flowers and cover with the same vinegar. Repeat after 2 weeks making a triple infusion in all.

An old Scottish recipe used half rosemary and half lavender to make a very refreshing vinegar for adding to 'Sweete Washing Water'.

Lavender footbaths are another very old-fashioned pleasure and made good use of lavender's ability to soothe the peripheral nerves, as well as its antiseptic qualitites and its clean sweet fragrance. A strong infusion of lavender flowers and leaves in boiling water was made. This was added to a basin of warm water in which the feet were allowed to soak blissfully at the end of a long day.

Sweet Water for Linens

This recipe is culled from *Bulleins Bullwarke* (1562):

Three pounds of Rose water, cloves, cinnamon, sauders[1], 2 handfull of the flowers of Lavender, lette it stand a moneth to still in the sonne, well closed in a glasse; Then distill it in Balneo Marial[2]. It is marvellous pleasant in savour, a water of wondrous sweetness, for the bedde, whereby the whole place shall have a most pleasant scent.

[1]Sandalwood
[2]Bain Marie or waterbath

Lavender oil and lavender flowers have long been recognised for their powerful insect repellent properties. Lavender was always an ingredient in moth repellent sachets to store among winter woollens. Here is my favourite mixture of dried herbs for moth bags which are made of voile or silk or organdie and tied with bows of satin ribbon.

Moth Repellent Sachet Mixture

2 cups dried lavender flowers
1 cup dried lightly crushed camphor laurel leaves
½ cup dried lightly crushed costmary leaves
1 cup dried wormwood leaves
½ cup dried pennyroyal
½ cup dried peppermint
1 cup dried lavender leaves

This fresh mint-and-lavender scent with astringent undertones really seems to keep the moths at bay. Hang a sachet on hangers and pop one in each drawer.

Lavender Wash Days

Plant a bush, or better yet a hedge, of lavender near the laundry door—French, Mitcham or English—and on sunny days dry lingerie and pillowslips over the bushes. An old tradition.

> We grew lavender in our old Maryland garden and the sheets in my Mother's house always smelled of it. What sweet slumbers come to one between Lavender-scented sheets!
>
> Louise Beebe Wilder, *The Fragrant Garden*

Store sheets fresh from the sun and wind with lavender bags between each folded sheet.

Lavender Insect Repellent

Lavender oil is a powerful insect repellent. Rub a few drops diluted in a little safflower oil on your skin before indulging in the great outdoors to repel flies, midges and mosquitoes. Or throw a handful of the dried stalks and branches left over from the harvest onto the barbecue or picnic fire. With stored fruit, sprinkle dried lavender leaves over it.

Lavender Furniture Polish

Old-fashioned beeswax-based furniture polishes really give a gleaming finish to wood and a fresh sweet country smell to a home. The same recipe can be used substituting rosemary or lemon verbena. Apply it sparingly and polish to a brilliant finish with a soft cloth.

½ cup (125 ml) water (distilled by preference)
1 large handful of English lavender flowers
25 g pure soap flakes
2 cups (600 ml) real turpentine
100 g pure beeswax
25 g white wax

Bring the distilled water to the boil in an enamelled or glass pot. Add the lavender and continue to boil for two minutes. Remove from the heat and allow to cool, then strain through a double layer of cloth and dissolve in the soap flakes. Place the waxes in separate pots in a roasting pan half filled with water and heat. Then pour both the waxes into a bowl, add the turpentine and the lavender infusion and beat all the ingredients together with a hand or preferably, electric beater until cool.

Lavender Liquid Polish

This liquid furniture polish really 'feeds' old wood and is easy to use when cleaning and polishing carved wood. Apply generously to dry wood, sparingly to well maintained wood and polish to a gentle clear shine with a clean soft cloth. The fragrance really permeates a room.

3 teaspoons oil of lavender (see recipe in the chapter 'Medicinal Lavender')
150 ml real turpentine
150 ml raw linseed oil
75 ml apple cider vinegar
75 ml methylated spirits
10 drops essential oil of lavender (optional)

Place all the ingredients together in a bottle and shake together thoroughly. Shake before using.

Lavender Talcum Powder

It is simplest to begin with a commercial unperfumed talcum powder, but arrowroot or cornflower can be used too.

Use a mortar and pestle to pulverise dried lavender flowers to as fine a powder as possible. Sieve through a fine mesh. Mix together equal quantities of sieved lavender and talcum powder or flour. Add a few drops of essential oil of lavender. Mix through thoroughly, sieve once more and bottle attractively.

Lavender Sweet Breath Lozenges

egg white
icing sugar
lavender oil

These sweet lavender pastilles were once most fashionable among ladies as a breath freshener after indulging in a little wine. A few drops of essential oil of lavender were added to well sieved icing sugar and mixed thoroughly. It was then bound with sufficient lightly beaten egg white to form a stiff paste, and small portions shaped into lozenge shaped pastilles. These were then set aside to dry and harden in a warm place. While these pastilles were an emergency social measure, a mouth wash made from an infusion of sage leaves was much favoured for everyday use, as was sage toothpaste.

Lavender Foot Rub

Finish off the good work done by a lavender foot bath with a soothing lavender foot rub. This recipe is particularly good for joggers or enthusiastic walkers, not only soothing tired muscles but helping to prevent blisters and adding moisture to the skin to prevent cracking.

½ tablespoon apple cider vinegar (no other)
*30 drops essential oil of lavender
*3 tablespoons of safflower or sunflower or avocado oil

*Both the essential oil and oil may be replaced by 3 tablespoons of your own oil of lavender if wished.

Mix all the ingredients together in a glass jar and stand in a roasting pan of hot water. Stir and heat gently. Allow to cool. Place cap on bottle and shake well. Remove the cap until the mixture is cold, then replace the cap. Shake before use.

Luscious Lavender Night Cream

1 tablespoon avocado oil or apricot oil
1 tablespoon almond oil
3 tablespoons lanolin
1 teaspoon oil of lavender (see chapter 'Medicinal Lavender')

If you work outside a lot this is the ideal answer to sore chapped hands and weatherbeaten skin. Put the lanolin in an ovenproof bowl and place in a roasting pan half full of hot water. Pour in the avocado and almond oil and beat well to completely combine. Remove from the heat and continue to beat as the mixture cools and thickens. Add the oil of lavender. Continue beating until mixture is thick and creamy and cool. Pour into a small pot, cover and store in the refrigerator. Vitamin E can be added by squeezing the contents of 2 or 3 capsules at the same stage as oil of lavender is added.

Lavender Ointment

Ointments, because they are thick and cling to the skin, hold active herbal extracts in prolonged contact to an area requiring treatment. In the old days lard was mixed with a herbal extract but petroleum jelly is a popular choice today. Put 200 g of petroleum jelly in a bowl and place in a roasting pan half full of water.

Melt the petroleum jelly, add two heaped tablespoons of lavender and continue to warm. Stir together thoroughly, then strain off the flowers through a double thickness of calico or similar undyed cloth. When cool, bottle into a wide mouth jar and store in the refrigerator to maintain the active principles.

Sweet Scented Armchair

In one of my favourite old books *Pot Pourri from a Surrey Garden* (1900), Mrs C.W. Earle described a delightfully fragrant household idea: 'On the backs of my armchairs are thin Liberty oblong bags, like miniature saddle-bags, filled with dried Lavender, Sweet Verbena and Sweet Geranium leaves. This mixture is much more fragrant than the lavender alone. The visitor who leans back in his chair, wonders from where the sweet scent comes.'

This is a Victorian elegancy developed from early ideas described by Parkinson in the seventeenth century of tying fragrant bundles of lavender, costmary and rosemary to 'lie upon the tops of beds'.

A more sophisticated way of dealing with the everpresent problems of moths in clothing was developed in the seventeenth century. Clothing was sprinkled with a fragrant concentrated moth-repellent liquid before being folded. Here is a seventeenth century recipe:

To make a special sweet water to perfume clothes in the folding being washed. Take a quart of Damask-Rose Water and put it into a glasse, put unto it a handful of Lavender Flowers, two ounces of Orris, a dram of Muske, the weight of four pence of Amber-greece, as much Civet, foure drops of Oyle of Clove, stop this close, and set it in the Sunne a fortnight; put one spoonfull of this Water into a bason of common water and put it into a glasse and so sprinkle your clothes with it in your folding.

8 Lavender Fragrance and Fancies

Making your own potpourri is a delightful hobby and easier than you may think...

The ancient and fragrant art of potpourri is one of the few truly civilised and civilising processes left for the twentieth century inhabitant to partake of. This 'preservation of garden souls' is a work worthy of time and loving care and its products can bring delight not only to the maker but to so many others.

We will disdain the often quoted and unworthy translation of the French 'rotten pot', and proceed hastily to the fact that there are two distinct techniques for potpourri production, 'moist' and 'dry'.

Moist potpourri is an old method of production and is presumably the source of the French title, for it is the fragrance, and most certainly not the appearance, that is the attraction with this variety. Moist potpourris are reputed to retain their fragrance for up to fifty years, so the process results in much longer staying power. They are made from floral materials that are partly dried, despite the name.

The peak time to pick any floral ingredient is just as it is coming into full bloom. Pick after the dew has dried but as early as possible on a sunny day. Dry the flowers on papers or preferably on screens, out of sunlight but in an airy place. For moist potpourri they should be only partly dried, leathery when finished rather than crisp. Aim for a very limp appearance. Around one third of their bulk will be gone.

We use large straight sided glazed pottery crocks with good fitting tops to hold and mature moist potpourris. These should really be set aside for the purpose as it takes a number of weeks to mature a batch. Never use metallic spoons to turn the mixture. Buy some long-handled wooden spoons and keep them for this purpose alone. To make your job pleasant the crock needs to be sufficiently large and wide-mouthed to hold all the ingredients comfortably during the necessary turnings and stirrings as the mixture ages. The shortest time needed to mature the mix is two weeks. This is really far too short. The best results come with longer maturation. We wait at least six to eight weeks, but in previous centuries, far more noted for their patience than our own, the crocks were left to stew for months.

The general principles are simple. Place a layer of 'leathery stage' petals at the bottom of the crock, then cover with a layer of common (not iodised) salt. Add another layer of petals, then salt, alternating them until the crock is about three quarters full. A batch requires at least two weeks ageing before the remaining ingredients are added. Weigh the mixture down with a plate on which is placed some heavy non-corrodable object. A large bottle of home-made preserves is an answer. A large glass jar filled with sand and tightly capped will do the job well too. Each day the mix needs to be stirred well from the bottom. A kind of 'petal soup' appears and should be mixed back into the petals. If a hard crust appears, remove it and allow it to dry. Reserve this for the final mixing when it should be crushed and added back.

Next the spices, ground roots, dried peels, fragrant leaves and fixatives are added and blended. Leave for one month, stirring daily and covering again, to mellow and mix the fragrances. Finally add whatever essential oils may be required and allow the mix to continue to 'stew' (the word is too appropriate to be avoidable), stirring daily, for a few more weeks.

If all this sounds tedious in the extreme, interrupting a very busy schedule, you are probably one of those who would most greatly benefit from its therapy! The fragrance alone is sufficient reward as the mixture is stirred each day, and it is no more difficult to build this routine into your day than any other daily routine.

Now is the time to move the potpourri into its final containers. Remember how long it will give pleasure to its owner and choose something worthy of the contents. Old Chinese ginger jars, oriental porcelain jars, even old-fashioned tea-caddies and marmalade jars in

fine pottery are suitable. Haunt second-hand and antique shops for suitable potpourri jars. The only provisos are that there is a solid cover and that it is made of glazed pottery of some kind. Once you are looking, it is amazing how many unusual and attractive old containers suggest themselves.

The mixture in its new container will still be a little raw in its quality of fragrance, but in a few weeks will be a delight. When you wish to scent a room, remove the cover and a delicious subtle fragrance will gently pervade the whole area. Otherwise keep the lid on the mixture.

Here are a few recipes for moist potpourri. Once you have mastered the basic technique you will be able to devise your own mixes.

A Thousand And One Flowers Potpourri

This is the perfect way to use that first delicious flood of fragrant flowers in spring.

Collect all the fragrant flower petals of the season: tea and other roses which should be the bulk of the mix; *Jasminum officinalis*, jonquils, orange and lemon blossoms and their shredded leaves, tuberose, *Acacia* blossom, clove pinks, lily-of-the-valley, honeysuckle, lilac, wallflowers, French lavender *(L. dentata)* which is the one flowering in spring, freesias and others. Follow the general principles described above, alternating the 'leather dry' petals and salt.

Once the initial ageing process is completed, the second round of ingredients can be added. These should include a good proportion of the following: eau-de-cologne mint, lemon verbena leaves, lemon balm leaves, sliced angelica root, peppermint, lemon scented and rose scented geraniums, bergamot leaves, ground clove-stuck orange peels, rosemary, lavender foliage, sweet marjoram. (To prepare the orange-and-clove mixture, cut thin peelings from oranges, lemons too if you like, so that they have no white pith. Stud with cloves and dry in a very slow oven until hard and completely dried out. Place in a mortar and pound to a powder. The fragrance is utterly delicious.) The roots and leaves should all be dry before adding. Also add cinnamon, powdered orris root, allspice, gum benzoin, a jigger of brandy, oil of rose geranium and oil of neroli.

Allow the mixture to go through its second maturation, then place in its final containers.

Old-Fashioned Brown Sugar Potpourri

This is an old recipe which is known to retain its fragrance for fifty years. Firstly prepare the bay salt. To 500 g common (non-iodised) salt, add ten (preferably fresh) bay leaves and pound in a mortar. Remove the remainder of the leaves when finished and the salt will have absorbed the pleasant fragrance of the bay. A number of the old recipes for moist potpourri contain this ingredient.

Take 16 cupfuls of 'leather-dried' rose petals. Measure the amount of salt calculated to cover the rose petals in alternate layers and prepare an equal quantity of brown sugar mixed thoroughly with allspice, nutmeg, cinnamon, 30 g orris root, and 125 g gum benzoin. To the rose petals add partly dried lavender flowers, whatever other 'leather dried' fragrant flowers you have to hand, together with semi-dried rose geranium leaves, lemon verbena and lemon geranium. Lemon or lime leaves are another suitable addition.

Alternate layers of the floral and leaf mixture with the bay salt and brown sugar mixture. Pour over a good wine glassful of brandy.

Mature as per the general instructions, stirring daily. When the mixture is fully matured place in its final containers.

Of course, as with all these recipes the quantities can be reduced or increased proportionately to cope with the supply of materials available to you.

A trick to remember for those who make lots of potpourri is that an electric coffee grinder can be used to readily powder dried citrus peels and spices. The problem is that a separate grinder from the one in which you grind your coffee is advisable as there may be carry-over flavour.

Dry potpourri is easier in a sense for all the ingredients can be gathered and dried separately as the season progresses. In this process each ingredient should be dried to crispness. Heat and light destroy fragrance and colour. Petals, leaves and flowers should be dried out of heat and sunlight but in a place with good air circulation. Petals may be dried thinly spread on papers or screens. Herbs, fragrant foliage and lavender spikes should be tied in small bunches hung upside down and well spaced from each other. Larger bunches are likely to mould and partially ferment inside, losing much of their fragrance and all of their colour.

I keep large glass storage jars with screwtop lids. Each ingredient as it dries is stored in its own container throughout the season. It is amazing how ingredients mount up with regular harvesting and drying. The jars are stored in a dark cool cupboard. Dried leaves should be stripped from their stems before storing. The exceptions with foliage are lemon verbena and eglantine rose leaves which I like to dry in the same manner as petals so that they retain a separate shape.

Many recipes call for dried pounded citrus peel or citrus and cloves. This can be prepared in quantity as described earlier and stored in a bottle for future needs. It is a good idea to keep a supply of whole spices for grinding.

Dry potpourri is designed to be not only deliciously fragrant but visually attractive. While the great majority of ingredients are included in dry potpourri for their fragrance, colour and decorative effect are important as well. Some non-fragrant flowers should be dried for

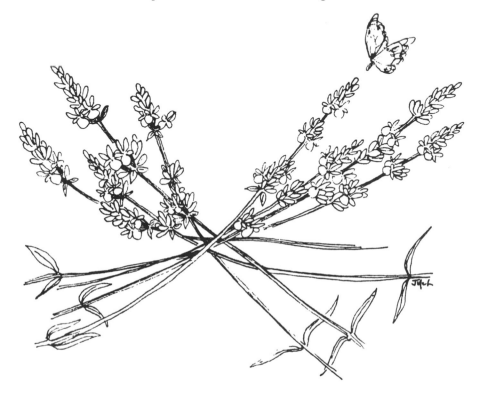

their ability to retain their bright fresh colours when dried. Individual florets of the annual statice, golden florets of tansy-leaf, dyer's chamomile flowers, tansy flowers, everlastings, flannel flowers (garden grown), calendula flower petals, cornflowers, borage flowers, delphinium flowers, bougainvillea flowers (marvellous!), coloured freesias and zinnia petals all look pretty. I prefer to press flannel flowers which are particularly beautiful, like white velvet starfish, and pressed pansies, heartsease and rose leaves are lovely decorations. The pretty double flowers of Parma violets and the double soapwort or pretty betsy are also delightful. I also like the flowers of the double wallflower and the double campions.

Dry potpourris do not have the longevity of fragrance that moist potpourris have. However they should last at least a year if properly prepared and many formulas last far longer. An old trick to revive a potpourri that is becoming faint is to add a jigger of brandy and stir it through.

As with moist potpourri, fixatives are essential to the longevity of the product's fragrance and the maintenance of the quantities of the fragrance. The most commonly used fixative in dry potpourri is orris root which has the advantage of a sweet violet fragrance. The easiest way to use it in dry potpourri is as dry chips. If the powdered form is used the essential oils should be mixed into it before incorporation with the other ingredients. Other useful fixatives are the various aromatic resins such as gum benzoin, storax, balsam of Peru and balsam of Tolu. The general proportion of fixative to mix is one tablespoon to four cups of dried petals and leaves.

Many other ingredients find their way into dry potpourri: lichens like oakmoss and reindeer moss, fine chips of perfumed woods like the sandalwoods, cedar and sassafras, the rhizomes of sweet flag and vetiver, and the pods of the vanilla orchid and Tonquin bean.

Dry potpourri is made in a single mixing then set aside in a securely closed container to cure for at least three and preferably six weeks.

Spices have some fixative qualitites in their own right. Cinnamon bark finely broken up, crushed cardamom seeds and mace are commonly included in the old recipes for this purpose as well as for their fragrance qualitites. Remember that dry potpourri intended for display in see-through containers such as glass jars should not contain powdered ingredients, either fixative or spice. Instead use fine chips and shavings, otherwise the surface of the container will be clouded over. People who suffer from hayfever often sneeze, not at the ingredients of potpourri, but because of finely powdered orris root and spices acting as an irritant. If either the maker of the potpourri or the recipient of it suffers from hayfever, it should be prepared with sliced and chipped ingredients rather than powdered whenever possible.

See through containers of various kinds can be used for dry potpourri. Often bowls are pretty but impractical. Even well-wrapped dry potpourri has a short life if constantly exposed over a wide surface area to the atmosphere, more so in hot summer months. Choose containers like old cut-glass or crystal jars from antique and second hand shops, enamelled boxes, and old-fashioned glass apothecary jars that are in vogue again. Then when you wish to scent a room it is an easy matter to lift the lid and allow the fragrance to permeate.

Potpourri is also a welcome gift in little fabric bags decorated with lace and tied with ribbons, or in little flat sachets of various shapes. For these powdered orris root can be used as clouding of the container is no longer a problem.

It is a mistake to use inferior oils for potpourri work. Buy the best quality you can find and possibly afford. The same obvious difference that is found between a top qualty perfume and a cheap one is also to be found between top quality oils and the cheap end of the synthetics.

Much time and love and effort goes into making potpourri and the result can be enjoyed for a very long time. Inferior quality oils can turn that pleasure into an endurance trial for everyone with even the most modestly discriminating nose. Expect to find quite a difference in costs of various grades of essential oils. Considerable difference will be found, too, between various types of oils. Some are rare and quite precious, others more easily obtained. This will be reflected in their price. Seal bottles very securely between uses and store in a cool dark place to prevent deterioration. A small quantity goes a long way and unless you are making huge quantities of potpourri your initial investment will last, treated well, for a long time.

Here are some recipes for dry lavender potpourri making use of a limited range of non-floral materials.

Summer Bowl

This recipe is based on a very ancient one little altered other than by translation:

4 cups dried red rose petals (preferably from fragrant old Gallica roses like 'Sissinghurst Castle', 'Duc de Guiche', 'The Apothecary's Rose', 'Charles de Mills', 'Tuscany Superb' or 'Surpasse Tout')
2 cups dried rose geranium leaves (*P. graveolens*, 'Attar of Roses', 'Dwarf Rose', 'Dr Livingstone', Round Leaf Rose)
2 cups dried lavender flowers
1 cup dried rosemary leaves
1 cup dried lemon verbena leaves
2 tablespoons each of ground allspice, ground cloves and finely broken cinnamon bark chips.
3 tablespoons orris root (chips are preferable to powder if the appearance of the potpourri is important)
3 tablespoons gum benzoin (pieces preferred to powder)
20 drops damask rose oil
10 drops lavender oil

Lavender Lace Potpourri

Mix together the following ingredients in the proportions by weight given:

8 parts dried lavender flowers
1 part dried thyme or lemon thyme
1 part dried sweet vernal grass or sweet woodruff
2 parts dried powdered orange peel
1 part oakmoss
1 part eau-de-cologne mint
1 part dried violet flowers
1 part dried southernwood
4 parts gum benzoin
1 part fine cinnamon bark chips

This old fashioned potpourri has a delicious woodsy scent like wild lavender. A few drops of essential oil of lavender may be added if wished.

Provencal Lavender Potpourri

4 cups dried rose petals
2 cups dried lavender flowers

1 cup dried orange blossoms
½ cup dried powdered orange peel
1 cup dried small-chipped orange or lemon leaves
1 cup dried violet flowers
1 cup dried small-chipped cinnamon bark
1 teaspoon ground cloves
1 teaspoon ground nutmeg
5 drops jasmine oil
20 drops oil of neroli

Summer Herbs Potpourri

4 cups dried lavender flowers
2 cups dried fragrant tiny pink roses (particularly good are 'Petite Lisette', 'Pompon Blanc Parfait', 'De Meaux', 'Spong', 'Petite de Hollande', 'Old Pink Moss', 'Little White Pet', 'Cornelia', 'Cecile Brunner', 'Blush Noisette', 'Orleans Rose', 'The Fairy', 'Dresden Doll', and 'Mignonette')
2 tablespoons dried Greek mountain oregano (incredibly delicious fragrance and silvery grey leaves)
2 tablespoons dried sweet marjoram
2 tablespoons dried sweet basil
2 tablespoons dried lemon thyme
1 cup dried rosemary needles and flowers
½ cup of dried southernwood
½ cup dried spearmint
1 cup dried lemon verbena leaves
12 drops oil of lavender
2 tablespoons orris root chips (or powdered orris root)

Cottage Garden Potpourri

1 cup dried lavender flowers
2 cups dried pink rose petals (preferably from extremely fragrant old Damask, Alba, Centifolia and Moss roses like 'Gloire de Guilan', 'Ispahan', 'Marie Louise', 'Petite Lisette', 'Quatre Saisons', 'The Rose of Kazanlik', 'Felicité Parmentier', 'Belle Amour', 'Fantin Latour', 'Old Cabbage Rose', 'Mme Louis Lévêque' and 'Gloire des Mousseaux')
2 cups dried lavender leaves
1 cup dried clove pink petals
1 cup dried rosemary leaves
2 cups dried rose geranium leaves (choose from 'Dr Livingstone', 'Dwarf Rose', 'Attar of Roses', 'Round Leaf Rose', *P. graveolens*)
1 cup dried blue delphinium flowers
2 tablespoons orris root chips
1 cup dried mignonette flowers
1 cup dried Westmoreland thyme
1 cup dried wallflowers
1 cup dried violets
1 cup sweet myrtle leaves
1 cup dried jasmine flowers

2 cups dried double hollyhock flowers
20 drops essential oil of lavender
20 drops essential oil of rose geranium
1 tablespoon coarsely ground nutmeg
1 tablespoon coarse ground cloves
6 quills cinnamon bark broken roughly into pieces

An Elizabethan Potpourri

6 cups dried damask roses
2 cups dried lavender
2 cups dried clove pinks
1 cup dried violets
1 cup dried pink paeony flowers
1 cup dried rosemary leaves
½ cup dried marjoram leaves
½ cup dried clary sage
½ cup dried costmary
½ cup sweet or white peppermint
1 tablespoon each of finely crushed cinnamon bark, powdered cloves, nutmeg and allspice
2 tablespoons orris root chips
1 tablespoon gum benzoin
5 drops essential oil of rose (damask preferred)
3 drops essential oil of sandalwood

After the usual curing time decorate bowls of this pretty and very fragrant potpourri with dried pink rosebuds and, if available, apple-scented pressed leaves of the eglantine rose.

Colonial Garden Potpourri

1 cup dried blue salvia flowers
1 cup dried blue hydrangea blossoms
1 cup dried clove pinks
1 cup dried rose petals

1 cup dried Queen Anne's lace
1 cup dried wallflowers
1 cup dried double yellow jasmine (*J. mesneyi*)
1 cup dried orange blossom
1 cup dried Balm of Gilead leaves
1 cup mixed dried bergamot leaves and flowers
1 cup dried larkspur flowers
½ cup dried sweet marjoram
1 cup dried lavender flowers
½ cup dried spearmint leaves
½ cup dried southernwood leaves
½ cup crushed dried sweet myrtle leaves
1 cup milfoil yarrow flowers
10 drops oil of rosemary
10 drops oil of roses
10 drops oil of bergamot
½ cup dried powdered orange peel
5 drops oil of neroli
⅓ cup orris root
½ cup small chipped cinnamon bark

Collect the various dry components during spring and summer and mix all the ingredients together in autumn. This mix looks gorgeous and smells fresh and delicious.

Potpourri Pour L'Homme

Men do not often get offered potpourri, yet a bowl of this for a study or office is fresh, delicious and clean...and most appreciated.

1 cup dried rosemary leaves
1 cup dried lavender flowers
½ cup dried chamomile
½ cup dried crushed pineapple sage leaves
½ cup dried peppermint leaves
½ cup dried lemon thyme leaves
½ cup dried southernwood leaves
¼ cup dried Balm of Gilead leaves
¼ cup dried spearmint leaves
1 cup dried sweet basil leaves
½ cup dried eau-de-cologne mint leaves
½ cup orris root chips
5 drops essential oil of rosemary
5 drops essential oil of rose geranium

Here is another potpourri traditionally made for men.

Citrus and Fir Potpourri

1 cup dried lavender flowers
1 cup dried flowers of pineapple sage or red bergamot flowers
1 cup eau-de-cologne mint

2 cups citrus leaves
½ cup purple basil *or* lemon basil
½ cup dried powdered orange peel
½ cup sandalwood chips
1 cup dried crushed balsam fir leaves
20 drops essential oil of lavender
10 drops essential oil of lemon
½ cup orris root chips

Lavender Incense

If you have a little incense burner, this is an easy incense to make and use. It is particularly useful in the sick room that has remained closed up for some time, quickly dispelling mustiness. Even better, it need cost nothing.

2 tablespons fine sawdust which has been sieved to remove coarse pieces
2 tablespoons finely crumbled dried lavender leaves and flowers
5 drops essential oil of lavender

Bath toiletries and cosmetics are another way of incorporating sweet lavender fragrance into your life.

Making your own soap is a great deal easier than many people imagine. Homemade soaps can be incredibly luxurious, rich, fragrant—and good for your skin! Making soap to save money is a very minimal goal. You should consider making soap because it is fun, because it is creative and because it opens up a whole new world of fragrance experiences—and yes, at the end of it all, you will save money.

Washing balls are a good way to start working with soap products. They are a very old idea. The washing balls are compounded of a finely grated pure quality unscented soap such as Castile, mixed with skin softening and aromatic ingredients.

Ipswich Balls were once very popular indeed. For 'almond cake' use 14 g of finely ground almond meal from your health food store or other suppliers. Oil of spike is lavender oil. Use a few drops of oil of musk or tincture of musk in place of the musk and ambergris in the recipe and you will have a creditable Ipswich Ball. Here is a famous recipe from *The Queen's Closet Opened* by W.M., Cook to Queen Henrietta Maria, published in 1655.

> Take a pound of fine white Castill Sope, shave it thin in a pinte of Rose-water, and let it stand two to three days, then pour all the water from it, and put to it half a pinte of fresh water, and so let it stand one whole day, then pour out that, and put half a pint more, and let it stand a night more, then put to it half an ounce [14 g] of powder called sweet Marjoram, a quarter of an ounce [7 g] of powder of Winter Savoury, two to three drops of oyl of Spike, and the oyl of cloves, three grains of Musk, and as much Ambergris, work all these together in a fair Mortar, with the powder of an Almond Cake dryed, and beaten as small as fine flour, so roll it round in your hands in Rosewater.

The final rolling in rosewater helps to smooth, polish and scent the ball. Let it stand for up to six weeks to harden otherwise the ball is used up too quickly. The soap is prevented from darkening if you add 14 g of powdered gum benzoin to the original recipe.

Here is the 'delicate washing ball' described in Ram's *Little Dodoen* in 1606:

> Take three ounces [85 g] of orris, half an ounce [14 g] of cypress, two ounces [57 g] of Calamus aromaticus, one ounce [28 g] of Rose leaves (petals), two ounces of Lavender flowers: beat all these together in a mortar sieving them through a fine sieve, then scrape some Castill sope, and dissolve

it with some Rose-water, then incorporate all your powders therewith, by labouring of them well in a mortar.

Form the mixture into small balls about the size of a large golf ball and set aside to dry thoroughly for six weeks.

It is possible to fashion all manner of fragrant soapballs based on finely grated Castile soap and incorporating finely ground cosmetic aromatic herbs, herbal oils and finely ground almond meal. The only limitation is one's imagination. Try this modern recipe to start with.

Lavender and Rose Washball

2 bars Castile soap (or any good quality pure soap) finely grated
rosewater
10 drops oil of lavender

Heat a quarter of a cup of rosewater and pour over the soap and allow to stand for 10 minutes. Work together very thoroughly, then incorporate the lavender oil. Set aside to begin drying out. After two days, form balls of soap between your hands and set aside to dry in the sun. When the balls have almost fully hardened moisten the hands with rosewater and polish each washball by rubbing between the hands. Now put aside for approximately six weeks to fully harden.

Washballs make delightful gifts wrapped in a square of tiny sprigged fabric tied with a satin ribbon.

Lavender Bath Cream

This recipe makes the bath water feel ultra soft, fragrant and luxurious, leaving the skin satiny and moisturised with no greasy residue on either you or the bath tub. Add ¼ cup to each bath tub when the water is adjusted to body temperature. Very hot water will curdle it like custard!

1 egg yolk
¼ cup almond oil *or* peach kernel *or* sesame oil
10 drops oil of lavender
10 drops oil of bergamot
4 drops oil of verbena
2 cups water

Place the egg yolk in the blender and whirl. Mix together the oil with the various essential oils and, with the blender on, gradually add the oil. Now turn the blender to high speed and add the water in a thin stream into the bowl.

If there is no blender to call upon, the same procedure will work with an egg beater or whisk—it's just tougher on the muscles!

The cream can be stored in the refrigerator for up to 3 weeks. Shake well before use.

Lavender Body Moisturising Cream

½ cup white beeswax (chips or grated from block)
3 tablespoons lanolin
12 tablespoons sweet almond oil
4 tablespoons distilled water
20 drops oil of lavender

20 drops oil of orange
10 drops oil of rosemary
10 drops oil of bergamot

Melt the wax chips in a double boiler over hot water, add the lanolin and blend, whisk together then slowly add the almond oil. Continue to whisk the mixture for a few minutes, then add the water a little at a time, still continuing to whisk. Remove from the burner and, while still whisking, add each of the essential oils. Store in a closed glass container.

Lavender Bath Moisturiser

Bath moisturisers leave the skin feeling silky smooth. Pat rather than rub dry with the towel to get the full moisturising effect. This one smells just like early morning with the dew on the herb garden.

3 tablespoons sesame oil *or* almond oil *or* safflower oil
3 tablespoons gum arabic powder from the chemist
1½ cups water
15 drops oil of lavender
2 drops of rose geranium

Place the gum arabic in a bowl. Blend the oil with the essential oil, then mix with the powder until a completely smooth consistency is reached. Place in a blender and, with the blender switched on high, gradually add the water in a stream to produce a rich silky emulsion. Store in a glass bottle and refrigerate. Allow to mature for two days before using.

Shake well before using and add ¼–½ cup to each bath.

Lavender Mist Bath Bags

Lavender has a relaxing effect on the peripheral nervous system and has long been used to treat headaches originating from nervous tension. Not surprisingly with these medicinal properties combined with its sweet clean smell, lavender has long been a consistuent of bath bags. These are made from squares of muslin or voile. A cupful of the mixture is placed in the centre of the square, the sides drawn up and tied into a bag with appropriate coloured ribbon.

½ cup dried sweet cicely
½ cup dried sweet woodruff
1 tablespoon dried valerian roots

¼ cup dried lavender leaves
½ cup dried lavender flowers
¼ cup dried angelica leaves
1½ cup medium ground oatmeal
½ cup almond meal
20 drops oil of lavender

Divide the mixture into 3 equal portions and tie into bags as previously described. Soak the bag thoroughly in hot water at the bottom of the bath before topping up with cool water. Squeeze the bag repeatedly until no more milkiness emerges. The water will now be silky soft and fragrant. Use the bag as a final gentle skin scrub. The bag is reuseable once provided it is used the next day.

Aromatic Bath

This recipe is adapted from the *Toilet of Flora* published in the seventeenth century. Combine half a cup of each of the following dried herbs: lavender, sweet marjoram, rosemary, thyme, bay leaves, wormwood, peppermint, pennyroyal, lemon balm. Add the mixture to two litres of water in an enamelled pan, boil for ten minutes, then allow to cool. Strain through a double layer of cloth and add half a bottle of brandy. Bottle. Add a little to the bathtub when bathing.

The Beauty Bath

Ninon de Lenclos was a celebrated and exceedingly beautiful French courtesan of the seventeenth centry. She died at the age of 85 (rare indeed at that time) and reputedly retained her smooth youthful skin and curves until the end. She attributed this to her special daily herbal bath. Here is her secret recipe.

1 handful crushed comfrey root
1 handful dried lavender flowers
1 handful dried mint leaves
1 handful dried rosemary leaves
1 handful dried Centifolia rose petals (recommended by famous French herbalist Maurice Messagué for its anti-wrinkle properties)

Mix together, tie in a muslin bag and place in a large bowl. Pour boiling water over the herbs and leave to steep for 20 minutes. Pour the resulting infusion into a warm bath, squeezing the bag hard to extract all the active principles.

An Eighteenth Century Sweet Bath

This bath would have been refreshing, antiseptic and deodorising.

1 cup dried rose petals
1 cup dried orange flowers
1 cup dried *Jasminum officinalis* flowers
1 cup dried bay leaves
1 cup dried mint leaves
1 cup dried pennyroyal leaves
1 cup dried citrus peel (yellow part only)
6 drops essential oil of lavender
6 drops essential oil of musk
6 drops essential oil rose geranium

Mix well and store in a glass jar. To use, tie 2–3 cups of the mixture in a muslin square, place in a bowl and pour boiling water over the herbs. Allow to infuse for twenty minutes, remove the herbs squeezing the muslin bag firmly to extract all the herb extract, and add this concentrated infusion to a warm bath.

The Ultimate Tranquility Bath

Save this bath until evening. You will find yourself unwinding wonderfully with this fragrant bath.

1 cup dried lavender flowers
1 cup dried linden flowers
1 cup dried chamomile flowers
1 cup dried valerian root chips
1 cup dried sweet marjoram
½ cup dried angelica leaves
½ cup dried lemon verbena leaves

Mix well together and use in the same way as the previous recipe.

Handwaters were a wonderful idea. They were added to the final rinse of delicate garments, used as a final hair rinse, or added to a basin of water when washing hands or face.

A traditional Scottish recipe used equal quantities of lavender, thyme and rosemary infused in wine.

Scottish Handwater

1 handful of lavender flowers
1 handful of thyme leaves
1 handful of rosemary leaves
1 bottle of still white wine

Place all the ingredients in the wine, cover, and allow to infuse in a warm place for two to three weeks. Strain and bottle attractively.

An old English recipe for sweet handwater is based on the simple Scottish recipe but is more complex in its ingredients and the final product was distilled. Here is an adaptation and translation.

English Sweet Handwater

6 handfuls fragrant Damask roses
2 handfuls rosemary
2 handfuls lavender
2 handfuls sweet marjoram
2 handfuls sweet basil
2 handfuls sweet balm
1 tablespoon cloves
2 tablespoons cinnamon bark chips
1 handful of bay leaves
Thinly sliced rind of two lemons
Thinly sliced rind of two oranges

Handful of flowering rosemary tops
White wine

Cover with white wine and leave in a warm place for 8 to 10 days. Distil off and bottle.

Lavender Bottles

19, 21 or 23 fresh supple lavender stalks in full flower
Lavender-coloured satin ribbon 0.5–1.0 cm wide

Tie the bunch of heads together tightly just below the flower spikes. One end of the lavender should be about 30 cm, the other as long as possible.

Gently turn all the stalks up around the bunch of flower spikes to make a cage. Tie the stems together above the flowers so that they are completely enclosed in a cage of green stems evenly spaced.

Use a bodkin (or thread onto a hairpin or use a safety pin) to weave the long end of the ribbon in and out of the stalks, working round and upward until the flowers are enclosed. The short end of ribbon should be brought down with the flower heads so that it is enclosed in the weaving. Now wind the long end several times around the stalks to secure them and finish with a bow of ribbon. I like to tie a second bow at the top of the stalks.

Dry the lavender bottles, preferably on drying frames in a well-aired, warm place out of direct light.

Lavender Basket

I began making these several years ago and they proved so popular that I have continued ever since. They can be of any size, from tiny cane baskets with handles up to substantial ones.

Lavender baskets are very fragrant as they are filled with dried lavender potpourri as a finish to the product.

Basket with handle
Dried whole stems of lavender flowers (French *L. dentata* looks great but English will look good if used generously)
Lavender potpourri
Oasis cut to fit the basket and reach half its height (florist supply shops are a source)
Florist wire
Dried stems of thyme, silver flowering stalks of wormwood, oregano flowering stalks, golden achillea flowers, dried pink rosebuds wired through the base, dried sprays of white baby's breath (gypsophila), pink everlasting daisies, dried sprays of silver lavender cotton, cream, pink and lavender statice, dried stalks of pink larkspur, or any other dried flowers and foliage you like

Loop the florist wire over the oasis and push through the basket to secure. Push the ends back into the basket neatly. Make sure the oasis is firmly fixed.

Arrange the dried foliage material in the basket to form a framework for the arrangement, making sure all pieces are securely embedded in the oasis. Now fill in with lots of dried lavender spikes which should predominate and a selection of golden or pink dried flowers to add colour. Gypsophila will give a lovely misty airy appearance to the basket.

Finally sieve lavender potpourri into the basket so that the oasis is well covered.

No two lavender baskets are the same, and they can be very individual expressions of their maker. A few drops of essential oil of lavender can be added to refresh the scent of the basket from time to time.

If you are doing a substantial pruning of large lavender bushes you can even fashion the basket itself from dried lavender twigs.

Lavender Fragrance Wreaths

Frame
Florist's wire
Fresh lavender flower spikes and fresh herb foliage eg. silvery artemisia, thyme, rosemary, lavender cotton, sweet marjoram etc. (Cut more than you expect to use.)

Frames for herbal wreaths vary according to tastes. You can make your own from a single circle bent from heavy gauge wire. This is then encircled with dry sphagnum moss, binding it on tightly and evenly to make a padded base for the wreath. Raffia or thick natural string are best for creating the herb base.

Frames can also be made from various vines such as grape, Japanese honeysuckle, wild clematis (which can reach pest proportions on our property, smothering valuable shrubs), or wistaria. Create the basic circle, then twine lengths of vine continuously in and out around the basic circle until it has reached the required thickness. Tuck ends into the wreath base as you go so that a neat but rustic effect is created.

Or visit your local florist for a wire frame which should then be bound with sphagnum as above, or a straw wreath base, or a professionally made grapevine base.

To obtain a professional appearance for the wreath, all materials need to swirl in the one direction. I prefer to work with fresh materials for the base and allow the wreath to dry almost completely before wiring or glueing on the flowers and other ornaments. Dried foliage is brittle to work with and it is far easier to work with the fresh flexible stalks of herbs. It's important to cut much more material than you imagine you will need. Wreaths positively swallow herbs.

Gather the chosen foliage material into numerous small bunches and begin wiring these to the frame with florist's wire. Spread each bunch over the frame carefully to cover it and overlap progressive bunches so that they will hide the stems of previous bunches. Continue swirling the material in the same direction until the frame is complete. Now tuck in extra sprigs of foliage all around the outside and inside edges, continuing to work in the same direction.

Small bunches of lavender are now wired into position in a swirl through the centre of the wreath. It can now be given to a friend as a fresh green herb and lavender wreath, or placed in an airy, cool, dimly lit place to dry and further decorate.

Dried lavender and herb wreaths can be further prettied up with small bunches of dried flowers like pink oregano, lavender mint and sage flowers, pink yarrow or pink and lavender statice, wired to florist's picks and arranged around the wreath to hide the stems. Tiny lavender potpourri bags secured with lavender ribbon can also be wired or glued into place.

Lavender Dolls and Lavender Mice

Lavender dolls are a pleasant pastime for rainy days, but you must first locate a source of old-fashioned wooden clothes pegs. Use a strongly lavender-scented potpourri and place it in an 8 cm wide circle of pretty sprigged cotton fabric. Tie onto the top of the peg with lavender satin ribbon to create the effect of a mob cap finished with a bow. For a truly professional effect, tie a bundle of some fine black or brown wool at one end to form a little wig on the top of the peg, and fasten it on with PVA glue. It can be plaited in various ways. Paint a face on the peg. Then tie on the mob cap of lavender when hair and face are fully dried.

Paint the base of the two prongs to imitate shoes. Then either paste on a simple wrap around cloak, or, if inspired to finer things, make a pretty little neck to ankles old fashioned dress with a lace ruff at the top.

The loveliest Lavender Mice by far that I have seen were being sold at the popular Salamanca Market held each week in Hobart in Tasmania. The upright body, made of grey felt, with a very pretty bewhiskered face was filled with fresh fragrant dried Tasmanian lavender. The mouse was finished with a lavender sprigged white cotton mob cap, lace-trimmed Victorian dress gathered around the neck and lavender ribbon. The effect was pure Beatrix Potter.

Lavender Drawer Liners

There are quick and easy ways of doing these, but for something very special try this version.

Lavender coloured poster paint
Silver green poster paint
Flowering spikes of lavender
Short sprigs of lavender leaves pressed for 2 to 3 days
Watercolour paper in appropriate sized sheets, around 140–170 g weight preferred
Lavender potpourri
Large plastic rubbish bin liner

The paper is decorated by means of flower and leaf prints. Squeeze out each paint into a separate saucer. Mix with a very little water to keep a reasonably thick consistency. Use a lavender head to do some practice printing on spare paper. Place one side of the lavender head in the paint, then press gently along its full length to obtain a print. If the paint is still too thick, or you press too hard, you will end up with a sludged effect and no details will show. Adjust the consistency of the paint with a few more drops of water if necessary. If it is too diluted it will flood the paper.

Print the pressed sprigs of leaves by placing on one side in the paint, placing on the practice sheet, covering with a second sheet of paper and gently pressing down.

When you are satisfied you have mastered the art of print painting with the leaves and flowers, design your own pattern of lavender sprigs and flowers across each sheet of watercolour paper.

Dry the sheets overnight, then place flat in the plastic bag with a good layer of lavender potpourri. Seal and store flat. After a month the paper will be fully impregnated with the scent.

If giving this paper as a present, roll and tie with lavender ribbon and decorate with a little bunch of fresh or dried French lavender flowers.

Lavender Tea Cosy

Nothing could be more old-fashioned or more deliciously fragrant than the warmth of a hot pot of tea releasing the fragrant oil of English lavender flowers.

Make a tea cosy from a flower sprigged cotton with wadding between the layers. Fashion two large pockets to line the two inside layers of the cosy. Place inside each pocket a large flat sachet of lavender potpourri. This way of making the tea cosy allows you to remove the old potpourri and replace with fresh when necessary. A pot of herb tea with the fragrance of lavender floating in the air is one of the most relaxing of indulgences in the middle of a tiring and busy day.

Lavender Candles

Candle wax (craft stores supply this)
Salad oil
Clean plastic yoghurt pots for moulds
Thin pointed wooden satay stick or similar
Wicking (available from craft stores)
Sticky tape
Pencil
Essential oil of lavender
Wax colouring (optional)

Coat the inside of the clean empty yoghurt pots with salad oil and pierce the base of each container to form a small hole in the centre with the satay stick. Suspend the pencil horizontally

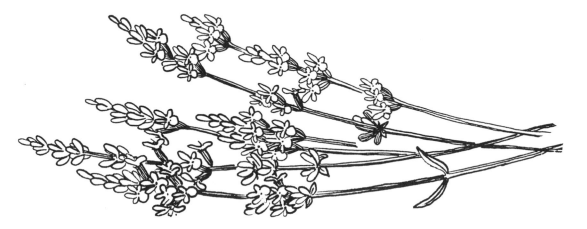

across the middle of a yoghurt pot, tie the wicking to the pencil so that it hangs centrally. Thread the wick through the bottom hole, cut the wick leaving about three centimetres projecting and pull taut holding it in position with sticky tape.

Warm the wax very carefully in a clean tin shaped to have a pouring lip, in a water bath. The wax is ready to pour into the mould when it reaches a temperature of 82°C (180°F). Stir in essential oil of lavender (10–15 drops per candle) and colouring if desired.

Pour the fragrant wax carefully into the mould being careful not to disturb the wick.

When the wax has hardened, tear away the mould, trim the wick and the candle is then ready for use.

Lavender Fans

These can be quite exquisite but should be treated as strictly ornamental and hung from a mirror or used to ornament a pillow or dressing table. They are better made as miniatures.

English lavender is freshly cut with long stems when approximately half the flower spike is open. Tie at the base of the bunch and about one third of the way up the stems.

Cut two pieces of lavender organza or lace into a fan shape to cover the upper two thirds of the lavender stems when gently teased out to form a fan shape. The lavender stems (I use pairs of stems for strength) form the ribs of the lavender fan. These are now sown into the lace casing, sewing both sides of each rib.

Press flat between books until dry and retaining their fan shape. Finish each little fan with lace and lavender ribbon bows, and wrap the satin ribbon tightly around the handle as a final touch, tying off with a bow and a sprig of dried French lavender.

9 First Eat Your Lavender

'Sweet not lasting. The perfume and suppliance of a minute, no more.'
Shakespeare

Today, flowers are planted in the garden strictly for their beauty. Yet not so long ago, violets and primroses, roses and carnations, chrysanthemums, lavender, calendulas, daylilies, clove gilliflowers, elderflowers, starry blue borage flowers, honeyed clover flowers and dandelion flowers were all included in everyday menus.

So too were the cottager's favourites: hollyhocks, fragrant gardenia petals, lilac flowers, jasmine, orange blossom and the blossom of lemons. In Germany the flowers of sweet woodruff were used. Rosemary and sage flowers were delicacies much favoured by ladies, and squash blossoms were an everyday summer delight stuffed with savoury mixes or deep fried in batter.

In this century the art of flower cookery was almost forgotten until the revival of interest in old-fashioned herbs and cottage flowers.

Lavender was a favourite flavouring in the cooking of Tudor and Elizabethan England, used as a relish to be served with game, roasted meats, with fruit salads, sprinkled over sweet dishes, or as a sweetmeat in its own right with the side benefit of relieving headaches!

Here is the recipe originally written by W.M., Cook to Queen Henrietta Maria, in *The Queen's Closet Opened* (1655).

Conserve of the Flowers of Lavender

Take the flowers being new so many as you please and beat them with three times their weight of White Sugar, after the same manner as Rosemary flowers; they will keep one year.

Later this recipe was varied a little to include a mixture of the fresh flower tops and green leaves. Of course it is the English lavender that was used in this recipe.

Flower conserves were delicacies for the ancient Greeks and Romans and were commonly served until the latter half of the nineteenth centuries as a relish for both meat and game. They were made from rosemary flowers, clove pinks, violet flowers, red rose petals and mint leaves.

Lavender conserve was the delight of Queen Elizabeth I. It was seldom absent from a table at which she sat. She also reputedly consumed countless cups of sweet lavender tisane which makes one hope that it was for pleasure and not for nervous tension headaches, for which it has been recommended since early times. The palace gardens were under the strictest instructions to have lavender flowers available at all times.

Sweet Lavender Tisane

Queen Elizabeth I reputedly consumed countless cups of this tisane.

3 tablespoons fresh English lavender flowers
2 cups boiling water
Honey

Allow the flowers to steep for 3 to 4 minutes, strain and serve with a slice of lemon and honey if liked.

If using dried flowers, halve the quantity used. A little mint or rosemary can be added for an interesting flavour variation.

The English long served their equivalent of the modern fruit salad with lavender flowers and on a bed of lettuce and lavender leaves. This is a delicious modern adaptation of that old idea.

Lavender Fruit Bowl

4 cups fruit cut into bite size pieces (Chinese gooseberries, whole canned lychees, whole hulled strawberries, whole stoned cherries, purple grapes deseeded, whole green sultana grapes, mango, orange)
1 cup lychee syrup
Juice of 1 lime
3 tablespoons Grand Marnier
1 cup sparkling wine
10 sprigs fresh lavender flowers

Chill together for several hours, gently blending together twice. When ready to serve, bring to the table decorated with fresh sprigs of lavender.

Sweet Lavender Fritters are an example of a favourite way of preparing flowers for dessert. Sprays of elderflowers, wattle flowers, rose petals and the spicily fragrant petals of clove pinks were all prepared in the same way.

Sweet Lavender Fritters

140 g melted butter
400 g flour
Good pinch baking soda
Yolk of an egg
2 egg whites
Pinch of salt
1 dessertspoon finely chopped fresh English lavender flowers

1 teacupful warm water
2 tablespoons lavender conserve

Beat all the ingredients except the egg whites to a creamy consistency and allow to stand
for at least one hour. When ready to use, fold in the two stiffly beaten egg whites. Heat a
light vegetable oil and add spoonfuls of the mixture. As each spoonful puffs up and turns
golden brown, turn with a slotted spoon. Drain on paper towelling.

Serve with a bowl of lemon wedges and a bowl of lavender conserve.

The addition of a tablespoon of brandy to the above recipe turns this into a very sophisticated
sweet.

Lavender and Apple Jelly is a great favourite at our Honeysuckle Cottage. Everyone who
tries it at our festivals does so with a rather tentative air, but is instantly converted at the
first taste. The jelly is not lavender coloured but a wine-rose colour, very pretty indeed. My
personal favourite is Lavender and Apple Jelly for scones, damper, and hot yeasty breads.
But a second sharper jelly is included here which is delicious to serve with meat.

Lavender and Apple Jelly

2 kg green unripe apples, roughly chopped
White sugar
½ cup dried English lavender flowers

Just cover the apples and lavender flowers in a pan with water and simmer until the apples
are soft and rather mushy. Strain the contents overnight through a jelly bag or equivalent.

Measure the liquid in cupfuls into a pan and add an equal quantity of sugar. Bring to
the boil and hold at a rolling boil until jellying point is reached. (Test with a couple of drops
on a cold saucer. Allow a short time then push gently at the drop from the side with a finger.
If the surface wrinkles, jellying point has been reached.) Pour the liquid into sterilised bottles
and seal.

Lavender Jelly

3 kg green apples, chopped roughly
Sugar
Juice of 4 lemons
1 cup lavender flowers
½ cup lavender vinegar *or* white wine vinegar

Place the apples, lemon juice, lavender flowers and vinegar in an enamelled or steel pan and cover with water. Bring to the boil then allow to simmer until the fruit is very soft. Strain the contents of the pan overnight through a jelly bag.

Measure the liquid in cupfuls into a pan and add an equal quantity of sugar. Bring to the boil and hold at a rolling boil until jellying point is reached. Pour into clean bottles and seal.

The jelly may be coloured with a few drops of green vegetable colouring if wished. A pretty touch is to place a head of clean dry fresh lavender in each jar before pouring the jelly in.

One of my favourite 'lavender foods' is Lavender Honey. It is the simplest of recipes to produce and tastes wonderful. Actually when the French or English Lavender is at its flowering peak in the garden, the honey produced by our bees has a delicious lavender scent and fragrance, quite unmistakeable. This recipe is a good approximation.

Lavender Honey

Honey (a light coloured one like clover or Patterson's Curse)
Dried English lavender flowers

Warm the honey gently in a double boiler. Add the lavender flowers and allow them to infuse. Remove from the heat and allow to stand in the sun (out of the way of ants) for a few hours. Strain out the lavender flowers and bottle. Lavender honey in a hot lemon drink is excellent for a sore throat as it is antiseptic. The honey is delicious on fresh crusty bread or wholemeal pancakes.

I had long made rosemary biscuits (and other delicious herb biscuits) but my introduction to Lavender Biscuits was at the First International Herb Conference, held in Melbourne. Our motel was less than ideal and I found myself breakfastless and about to present a one hour paper on the old herbal roses. A very kind lady pressed upon me a cup of hot tea and a bag of Lavender Biscuits from the Yuulong Lavender Estate. They were delicious! And a tired (the disco downstairs had reverberated for hours the previous night) and hungry speaker, immensely revived and restored, was able to breeze through an hour's talk.

Here, thanks to Edythe Anderson and Rosemary Holmes, owners of Yuulong Lavender Estate, is the recipe for those delicious biscuits.

Lavender Biscuits

125 g (4½ oz) butter or margarine
100 g (4 oz) sugar
1 egg
150–200 g (5–7 oz) self raising flour
1 level tablespoon dried English lavender flowers *(Lavandula angustifolia)*. It is essential to use English lavender with no camphor scent.
1 small cup chopped glacé ginger (optional)

Cream butter and sugar, add egg and beat well. Add dried English lavender flowers and mix well. Include ginger here if required. Finally add sieved self raising flour and mix all together.

Place teaspoonfuls onto a baking tray lined with non-stick baking paper and bake in a pre-heated moderate oven for about 15–20 minutes. This makes approximately 30 biscuits.

And, for good measure, this is the recipe for the equally delicious Yuulong Lavender Mustard.

Yuulong Lavender Mustard

150 g packet yellow mustard seed
150 g packet black mustard seed
20 whole cloves
1 tablespoon chopped fresh tarragon
1 tablespoon chopped fresh thyme
¾ cup parsley sprigs
2 inch piece of green ginger
3 cloves garlic
4 dessertspoons honey
3 dessertspoons salt
1½ cups of white wine vinegar
1 cup olive oil
3 dessertspoons of lavender

Combine the mustard seeds and cloves in a blender, add tarragon, thyme, parsley, peeled ginger, peeled garlic, honey and salt. Process until ingredients are finely chopped and gradually add vinegar and oil while continuing to process. Cover, stand overnight, then add lavender. Stir in thoroughly with a wooden spoon. If a smooth mustard is required process a second time.

Lavender and Lemon Icing

Lavender and lemon combine fragrantly as an icing for small plain cakes. Pound finely chopped lavender flowers with icing sugar to release the fragrant lavender oil. Cover and store for at least a week to allow the fragrance to permeate the icing sugar. When required, mix the icing sugar with fresh lemon juice to make a thin icing to spread on cakes or biscuits. A little finely grated zest of lemon can be mixed in. A large quantity of lavender icing sugar can be made up in one batch and stored for several months.

Lavender Vinegar

John Evelyn himself would have approved the use of this vinegar in his 'salets'. We used it on a tossed mixed green salad with plenty of herbs, shredded nasturtium flowers and shredded young violet leaves. Use a wide mouthed glass jar with a plastic or glass top. Half fill the jar with lightly packed-down lavender flowers and leaves that are gathered when all the dew has dried. Fill the bottle with a good white wine vinegar or cider vinegar. Place the cap on and allow to infuse in the warmth of the sun for two or three weeks shaking from time to time.

Strain and store in plastic or cork topped bottles (never metal). Use this as the basis of a French salad dressing.

Sweet Lavender Oranges

6 large sweet seedless oranges
3 tablespoons Grand Marnier or Cointreau
1 cup raw sugar
1 cup water
1 tablespoon finely chopped fresh lavender flowers

Finely peel off the orange part of the skin leaving behind the pith. Slice the peel into fine long slices. Place in a pan with the sugar, water and lavender flowers. Boil to form a syrup and cool. Add the liqueur. Remove the pith from the oranges and slice thinly into rounds. Place in a serving dish and pour over the cooled syrup. Chill for one to two hours. Serve garnished with fresh lavender flowers and mint leaves.

Other sweet thoughts for lavender? When making an apple crumble, mix one tablespoon of fresh lavender flowers with the apples and replace the sugar with lavender conserve. Baked apples are even more delicious if the stuffing used to replace the core includes a little fresh green ginger and lavender flowers. When making apple fritters sprinkle with lavender conserve rather than sugar before serving.

10 Medicinal Lavender

His Aunt Jobiska made him drink
Lavender water tinged with pink
For she said, 'The world in general knows
There's nothing so good for a Pobble's toes!'

Edward Lear, 'The Pobble Who Has No Toes'

The old herbals constantly sang the praises of lavender for medicinal purposes. John Gerard wrote in his *Herball* (1597):

> The distilled water of Lavander smelt unto, or the temples and and forehead bathed therewith, is refreshing to them that have the Catalepsie, a light migram, and to them that have the falling sickness and that use to swoune much.
>
> The floures of Lavander picked from the knaps, I meane the blew part and not the husk, mixed with Cinnamon, Nutmegs, and Cloves, made into pouder, and given to drinke in the distilled water thereof, doth helpe the panting and passion of the heart, prevaileth against giddinesse, turning, or swimming of the braine, and members subject to the palsie.
>
> French Lavander hath a body like Lavander, short, and of woodie substance, but slenderer, beset with long narrow leaves, of a whitish colour, lesser than those of Lavander; it hath in the top bushie or spikie heads, well compact or thrust togither; out of the which grow foorth small purple flowers, or a pleasant smell. The seede is small and blackish: the roote is harde and woodie.

But long before physicians like Gerard wrote of the virtues of lavender it had been highly regarded for its medicinal uses. Dioscorides wrote in 60AD:

> Stoechas grows in the islands of Galatia over against Messalia, called ye Stoechades, from whence also it had its name, is an herb with slender twiggs, having ye haire like Tyme, but yet longer leaved, & sharp in ye taste, & somewhat bitterish, but ye decoction of it as the Hyssop is good for ye griefs in ye thorax. It is mingled also profitably with Antidots.

Lavenders from the only known
edition of Dioscorides, Venice, 1558

lavender and hyssop seem to have been used in similar ways. The *Agnus Castus* of the 14th century made the same comments as those of Dioscorides some 1300 years later:

> Lavandula is an herbe men clepe lavandre. This herbe is moche lyk to ysope but it is mo lengger lewys thenne ysope and it hast a flour sumdel blew and also the stalke growith other-wyse. The vertu of this herbe is ef it be sothyn in water and dronke that water it wele hele the palsye and many other ewyls.

lavender was once a virtual medicine chest in every home. It was used for everything: as a nerve stimulant and restorative, for the relief of muscular aches and pains and sprains, to induce peaceful slumber and ease the ache of rheumatism and nervous headaches, to promote the appetite following illness, and to relieve flatulence.

Merck said of true lavender *(L. angustifolia)* that it was 'a stimulant, tonic, and used internally and externally in hysteria, headaches, fainting, nervous palpitation and giddiness'. The 'vapours' so beloved of susceptible Victorian ladies were frequently treated with lavender water. No doubt loosened stays contributed to the cure!

As has so often occurred when old herbal remedies have been tested by modern science, many of lavender's medicinal uses have been found to be solidly based in fact. Lavender oil has been shown to have antibiotic activity and will kill pneumonococcus, streptococcus, Koch's bacillus, diphtheria and typhoid bacilli. So the traditional use of oil of lavender in the treatment of mild burns, abrasions, cuts, sword wounds, sores, varicose ulcers and stings, and also for coughs, colds and chest infections with a lavender tisane or steam inhalation, would have been effective. I've even used lavender cologne as an antiseptic when delivering a litter of Burmese kittens! An infusion of the flowers of true lavender was also used as a douche for leucorrhoea.

Lavender oil was used extensively as an antiseptic in World Wars I and II when surgical supplies became scarce. Lavender farms, herb farms and every grower of a lavender bush in England were asked to contribute lavender for this cause. Britain, cut off from Continental sources of much needed drugs, appeals to its citizens to assist the war effort by gathering various herbs from the seashore and countryside. Among the herbs requested in World War II were foxgloves, comfrey, wormwood, marigolds, yarrow, elderflowers and hawthorn berries from the hedgerows and woods, and seaweeds rich in agar from the coast. Some 750 tonnes of dried herbs were gathered by the Women's Institute, Girl Guides, Boy Scouts and men and women in the various services. And should that quantity not sound vast enough, the quantity of fresh herbs required to produce that amount of dried herbs was 6000 tonnes!

In France, it is still quite common for housewifes to keep a bottle of essence of lavender for use on bruises, sprains and bites.

Anyone who has stripped dried lavender flowers from their stalks on a warm summer day in a fairly closed room will know that the temptation to fall asleep is utterly irrisistible. Its sedative action is amazingly strong and often, by just opening a bottle of oil in a confined space, I have seen visible relaxation in a person who is very anxious or stressed.

A weak infusion (5 g of dried flowers in a litre of boiling water) sweetened with honey was a traditional treatment for problems of nervous origin such as insomnia, irritability and nervous headaches. A few drops of oil of lavender rubbed on the temples was considered equally effective. And if your sleeplessness is of the tossing and turning variety compounded by summer heat, try my favourite trick of sprinkling the pillow with cool fragrant lavender water. It is as amazingly effective as it is old-fashioned. Sleep pillows containing fresh dried lavender are the answer for those who make a habit of seeing the dawn in.

Rosemary Hemphill, an expert on herbs and author of many well-known books on them, told me that a rub-down of lavender oil before retiring to bed completely relieved night-time symptoms of constantly spasming leg muscles, which is a truly exhausting condition to suffer from. For those with weary legs at the end of a hard day's work, a few drops of oil of lavender in a hot footbath can relieve fatigue remarkably. A few drops of oil rubbed into the skin has also been used traditionally to ease neuralgic pain. And an old countryman's trick in both England and France was to tuck a spray of lavender under a hat to prevent or cure a nervous headache.

I have used lavender oil diluted in baby oil and rubbed on the skin as a treatment for the excruciating pain of herpes minor around the side and back of the body. It was the only treatment that offered real relief in this instance to the victim and a reasonable sleep at night, and was rubbed over the affected area an hour before retiring. Lavender water rubbed on the back and chest can, in my experience, do much to quieten irritating chest coughs and has traditionally been used for this purpose in France. Lavender is sedative to both the nervous system and the respiratory tract.

One use of lavender that I automatically dismissed was in the treatment of snakebite. In the south of France, immediately rubbing the puncture wounds with a bunch of wild lavender was a standard anti-venom treatment. Hunters in Provence carried bunches with them as a precaution. The area has its fair share of poisonous snakes, particularly vipers, and hunting dogs often encountered them. Does it work? I don't know, but great modern French herbalists such as Maurice Mességué, who wrote from considerable first hand experience of this usage, and Jean Palaiseul write of its remarkable neutralising powers against venom. The usage is in any case long established. St Hildegard, the Benedictine abbess, a very learned woman, devoted a chapter to the medicinal and anti-venom uses of lavender in her famed medical treatise, and Salmon in his *Herbal* (1710) particularly mentions this usage.

Compound tincture of lavender or tincture of red lavender was listed in the British Pharmacopoeia for over two hundred years. It was known in the eighteenth century as Red Hartshorn or Palsy Drops. The early formulation was a complex one involving the distillation of lavender flowers, sage flowers, rosemary flowers, cowslips, betony flowers and others with French brandy. A maceration was then prepared from the distillate and various aromatic spices. Finally fixatives, colourants and fragrance were added in the form of the Apothecary's Rose (*R. gallica officinalis*), musk, ambergris, saffron and red sandalwood. The 1746 Pharmacopoeia saw a considerable simplification in the formulation, consisting of the oils of rosemary and lavender added to spirits of wine and macerated with nutmeg, cinnamon and red sandalwood. This formulation remained virtually unchanged thereafter.

Red lavender lozenges were also favoured as a mild stimulant against faintness and giddiness. Other traditional formulations included the famous Oleum Spicae, which consisted of one part of oil of lavender and three parts spirits of wine and was popularly used on sprains and stiff or aching joints. Pure oil of lavender was once commonly used rubbed into paralysed legs to stimulate them. I imagine that in cases of hysterical paralysis caused by trauma of various kinds it might well have been very effective.

The volatile oil obtained from distillation of *L. angustifolia* contains lavenderyl acetate, terpineol, pinene, borneol, camphor, cineole, linabol, limonene and linalyl acetate.

Spike lavender oil or aspic lavender oil, distilled from *L. latifolia* and various forms of lavandin, contains an oil rich in cineole and camphor and has a penetrating camphoraceous odour. It finds some use in veterinary practice, particularly on the Continent, in the control of external parasites and as a vermifuge.

Spanish lavender oil, which is distilled in Spain, has a chemical composition resembling that of spike lavender oil. *L. stoechas* (Italian lavender) is similarly distilled and is likewise low in the esters present in *L. angustifolia*. They are used to add fragrance to soaps, disinfectants and other household items, in the manufacture of some fine varnishes and lacquers and by porcelain painters.

While its medicinal use appears to be restricted to veterinary practice, there is a traditional use of spike lavender oil in promoting the regrowth of hair that is falling out. Where the problem is of nervous origin there may well be a particular basis for such a tradition. Lavender also had a reputation as a stimulant to the scalp. Arab women have traditionally used a lavender and basil based tonic to perfume and strengthen their hair. To make it, mix together in a glass bottle 2 cups of vodka, 30 ml lavender water, 30 drops of essential oil of lavender and 30 drops essential oil of basil. Allow to mature for two months, shaking thoroughly at regular intervals.

Even the 'straw', the stems of dried lavender after the flowers have been stripped, has found medicinal use, being burned in bundles as a deodorant and disinfectant of sick rooms.

Many lavender products are available on the market, but if you grow your own lavender it is possible to make up some of these old-fashioned fragrant formulas for yourself. Be sure to use English lavender *(L. angustifolia)*.

Oil of Lavender

This is not the commercially distilled essential oil, but a rubbing oil which can be used at full strength. (Essential oil of lavender obtained by distillation of fresh lavender flowers should be diluted in light vegetable oil for use as a massage oil when needed.)

To make oil of lavender, take a clean glass bottle and add to it a good large handful of fresh lavender flowers and cover with one litre of olive oil. Cover and leave to macerate in the warmth of the sun for three to five days. Strain through a cloth, add fresh flowers to the bottle and return the lavender-infused oil. Repeat until the oil is highly perfumed and charged with the active principles of lavender.

Lavender Water

Of course this can be bought commercially. My favourite comes from Norfolk Lavender in England. But for home purposes you can enjoy making up your own supply. In a clear glass bottle steep 100 g of lavender flowers in half a litre of alcohol (brandy or vodka are both good). Place in the sun for a few days, then strain. Repeat until the fragrance is very strong.

Strain and seal in a glass bottle. If your hair is weak, falling out and breaking, try an old idea and rub lavender water into your scalp several times a week. Try it too as a rub for rheumatism. It has a long tradition of usage for both problems.

Lavender Antiseptic Wash

This was a favourite treatment for eczema, cuts, acne and minor burns. Take a good handful of the flowers and boil together with half a litre of water for ten minutes. Filter and allow to cool before using. Since Roman days this has been used in hot baths, to relax the body, and it is known to have a marked effect on the peripheral nervous system. It has also been widely used as a gargle for sore throats and sore or infected gums, due to its antiseptic properties and relaxant effect on the nervous system.

Lavender Water for Fever and Headaches

2 tablespoons dried lavender flowers
1 tablespoon Sweet Cicely
1 tablespoon marjoram
1 tablespoon red rose petals
1 teaspoon cinnamon
1 large pinch ground cloves

Powder all the ingredients as finely as possible and mix with four cups of either surgical spirit or brandy. Allow to steep for 14 days, strain and bottle, sealing tightly. Add a few drops to cold water, wring out a towel in the liquid and place on the forehead. Repeat until relief is obtained.

In my experience, a sachet of the same mixture makes an excellent portable headache reliever.

In the once Imperial Library of Hungary lies a handwritten manuscript inscribed long ago by Queen Elizabeth of that country and dated 1235. In it is written the original prescription

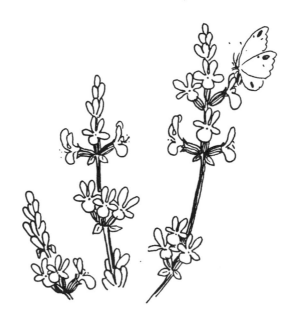

for the famous Hungary Water. The Queen was paralysed, but was cured by a secret herbal recipe invented for her by a hermit. The preparation was rubbed each day into her limbs and eventually restored her. The Queen's formula for Hungary Water became well known throughout Europe and was particularly widely used in southern France. The original recipe given here is on a queenly scale but can of course be made in much smaller quantities.

Hungary Water

1 gallon brandy or clear spirits (equal to 16 cups)
1 handful of rosemary
1 handful of lavender
1 handful myrtle

Handfuls are measured by cutting branches of the herbs twelve inches long. A handful is the number of such branches that can be held in the hand. After measuring, the branches should be cut up into one-inch pieces, and put to infuse in the brandy. You will then have the finest Hungary Water that can be made.

Many people who have bought lavender-based herbal sleep pillows from us have reported not only overcoming insomnia but that they were helpful in cases of asthma, and particularly in breaking up pulmonary congestion. The ingredients of sleep pillows vary but it is important to make the mixture around 3 parts of dried lavender flowers and leaves. The fourth part, made up of various tranquillising or sleep inducing herbs, can be mixed in different proportions according to what you have available.

Lavender Sleep Pillow

Mix together the following ingredients:

3 parts of lavender flowers
Hop flowers or lemon verbena leaves
Rosemary leaves
Marjoram leaves
Sweet Cicely leaves
2–3 drops lavender oil

Sew the mixture into a bag made of thin material which will allow the fragrance to escape eg. organza or muslin. Make a pillow slip to contain the sleep pillow. Silks are ideal.

Lavender used as an inhalant was considered in the past to speed recovery from colds, bronchitis, tonsillitis and flu.

Lavender Inhalant

Make a hot infusion of one good handful of lavender in 3½ cups of water. Add a few drops of oil and inhale the steam under a cloth. If you wish, add one or more of the following: thyme, sage or peppermint.

As an alternative, you might like to try William Turner's suggestion from the *New Herball* (1551):

I judge that the flowers of Lavender quilted in a cap and worne are good for all diseases of the head that comne from a cold cause and that they comfort the braine very well.

Four Thieves Vinegar

This antiseptic vinegar is attributed to a gang of four thieves who robbed the bodies of victims of the plague in Marseilles in 1722. They washed their bodies with it, frequently disinfecting their hands, and sprinkled it on their clothes and around their houses. It is said that all four survived without infection.

Actually it is not surprising that this famous aromatic vinegar was so successful. Many of its ingredients are among the most powerful natural antibiotics in the world. Another case of empirically gained knowledge long preceding that obtained by scientific investigation.

Infuse garlic cloves, lavender flowers, rosemary, sage, calamus root, mint, wormwood, rue, cinnamon, nutmeg and cloves in a glass flagon of wine vinegar and leave sealed in the sun for 3–4 weeks to release the powerfully antibiotic oils into the vinegar. Filter, pour into smaller bottles, add a little camphor and seal until ready for use.

Lavender Cream

This is an antiseptic cream and has been traditionally used for all manner of minor cuts, abrasions, bruises etc.

125 g white wax
500 g sweet almond oil
370 g distilled water
10 g essential oil of lavender
2.5 g spike oil

Lavender Ointment

25 drops essential oil of lavender
10 drops essential oil of lemon or neroli
5 drops essential oil of thyme
2 tablespoons oil of lavender (see recipe this chapter)
60 g pure beeswax

Warm the beeswax in a small pot in a roasting pan of hot water and, when melted, beat in the oil of lavender; then, as the ointment cools, add the essential oils, continuing to beat until cool. Store in a covered jar in the refrigerator.

Soothing Massage Oil

⅓ cup safflower or sunflower oil
Dried pot marigold petals
12 drops essential oil of rose geranium
12 drops essential oil of lavender
10 drops essential pine oil *or* oil of cypress

Place the safflower oil in a glass jar and add as many freshly dried pot marigold petals as possible. Cap the bottle and place in the sun for 4–5 days. Filter off the petals and squeeze out any retained oil from them before discarding. The oil will now be deep orange and fully charged with the active healing principles of calendula. Mix the other essential oils into the infused oil of marigold, bottle and store in the refrigerator.

11 Lavender Cries of London

In the busy streets of London no itinerant trader could afford to be modest about the wares he offered. Bakers and milkmen, fishmongers with fresh oysters and eels, and chimney sweeps, flower sellers and hot chestnut sellers, all had their own stock phrases describing their services or produce that they would call endlessly to capture attention. They were first recorded by John Lydgate, a Benedictine monk, in the fifteenth century and have been part of the folklore of London every since.

The lavender cries must surely have been among the first, as lavender was appreciated early for its fragrance and household uses, but the first printed record dates from c.1700 in *The Cries of London*, which included other much used and sold herbs like sage and thyme, rosemary and mint.

In *English Country Songs* (1893), edited by Lucy E. Broadwood and J.A. Maitland, the most familiar lavender cry of all was first recorded

> Will you buy my sweet lavender,
> Sweet blooming lavender
> Oh buy my pretty lavender
> Sixteen bunches a penny.

Inflation was later to convert this to 'Sixteen bunches a shilling'. Each lavender seller had her own version. Another was:

> Will you buy my sweet lavender, lady?
> Only 16 bunches for a penny,
> You'll buy it once, you'll buy it twice, lady,
> It'll make your clothes smell, oh, so very nice.

Most plaintive perhaps was:

> Lavender! Sweet Lavender!
> Who'll buy my sweet Lavender!

This was even further shortened to

> Buy my Lavender! Sweet blooming lavender!

or

> Won't you buy my sweet lavender.

A great deal more muscular in tone was:

> Sixteen good bunches a penny! Blooming lavender.
> Blooming lavender!
> Who'll buy sixteen good bunches a penny?
> Blooming lavender! Lavender!

That one I can almost hear Eliza Doolittle's father bawling. By the 1890s this was reduced to

> Sweetly blooming Lavender, sixteen branches a penny!

Another authorative call was

> Lavender! Sweet blooming lavender,
> Six bunches for a penny today!
> Lavender! Sweet blooming lavender,
> Ladies, buy it while you may.

and

> Here's your sweet lavender,
> Sixteen sprigs a penny,
> Which you'll find my ladies,
> will smell as sweet as any.

Mitcham lavender had a special clout in its day and some sales cries made a point of mentioning it by name. Perhaps the best known of these cries, recorded in a 1919 edition of the *Journal of the Folk Song Society*, was:

> Ladies, come, make no delay
> My lavender fresh cut from Mitcham, and I am round here today.
> Ladies buy a pennouth of my lavender
> There are 16 good branches a penny, all in bloom.
> Some are large and some are small;
> Take 'em in, show 'em all,
> There's 16 good branches a penny, all in bloom.

Many songs, too, were written about lavender. The most popular, one that every child knows as a nursery rhyme, is 'Lavender Blue' which has many versions. It originated c.1805 and was revamped as a popular song sung by Dinah Shore in 1948.

> Lavender's blue, diddle diddle,
> Lavender's green;
> When I am king, diddle diddle,
> You shall be queen.

This early nineteenth century rhyme had its beginnings in a late seventeenth century broadsheet:

> Lavender's green, diddle diddle,
> Lavender's blue
> You must love me, diddle diddle,
> Cause I love you.
> I heard one say, diddle diddle,
> Since I came hither
> That you and I, diddle diddle,
> Must lie together.

A different version of the nineteenth century rhyme was:

> Lavender blue and Rosemary green,
> When I am king you shall be queen;
> Call up my maids at four o'clock,
> Some up the wheels and some to the rock;
> Some to make hay and some to shear corn,
> And you and I will keep the bed warm.

Another very pretty song recorded in a book called *London Melodies* published in 1812 is:

> Come buy my lavender, sweet maids
> You cannot think it dear;
> There must be profit in all trades,
> Mine comes but once a year.
>
> Just put one bundle to your nose,
> What rose can this excel;
> Throw it among your finest clothes,
> And grateful they will smell.
>
> Though Winter come, it still retains
> The fragrance of today;
> And while the smallest part remains
> Your pocket will repay.
>
> One penny's worth is all I have,
> This sold, my stock is done;
> My weary footsteps you might save
> By purchasing this one.

What nostalgia the cries and songs can evoke. *Chambers Journal* of 11 August 1894 records the meaning of the cries to Londoners:

> When summer is nearly past, and autumnal tints are just beginning to appear, the call of 'Sweetly blooming Lavender, sixteen branches a penny!' is one

of the familiar street cries of London and other of our cities. The call reminds us of the near approach of the colder, darker days; but it also brings up thoughts of one of the sweetest of all floral perfumes.

The lavender sellers themselves were a mixture of growers selling their own wares and gypsies who long had an association with Mitcham. The gypsies often made up lavender bags for sale as well as fresh lavender. The bags could be placed in drawers between fresh linen, hung to perfume and ward off moths in wardrobes, or tucked into clothing where body warmth released its sweet fresh scent.

Hawkers were forbidden by law to knock on doors to sell their wares. The various cries were invented as an alternative means of attracting attention to their produce. Time turned a necessity into a much-loved tradition of the city. And as the refrain of *The Cries of London* said:

> Let none despise the many, many cries,
> Of famous London town.

. . .nor the most homely but perhaps most evocative and best loved of all flowers, gentle, enduring, old-fashioned lavender.

Further Reading

Angel, Marie. 1980. *Cottage Flowers*. Pelham, London.

Bremmess, Lesley. 1988. *The Complete Book of Herbs*. R.D. Press.

Brierley, W.B. 1916. *A Phoma Disease of Lavender*. Kew Bull.

Brown, Deni. *Fine Herbs*. Unwin Hyman, London.

Brownlow, Margaret. 1978. *Herbs and the Fragrant Garden*. Revised edition. Darton, Longman and Todd.

Clarkson, Rosetta E. 1940. *Green Enchantment: The Magic Spell of Gardens*. Macmillan. Republished 1972 as *The Golden Age of Herbs and Herbalists*. Dover, N.Y.

Culpepper, Nicolas. 1979. *Complete Herbal and English Physician*. Facsimile edition from the original 1826 edition. Gareth Powell, Hong Kong.

Cunningham, Scott. 1985. *Magical Herbalism: The Secret Craft of the Wise*. Llewellyn Publications, Minnesota.

Dawson, Warren R. 1934. *A Leech Book, or, Collection of Medicine Recipes of the Fifteenth Century*. London. 1934.

Earle, Mrs C.W. 1900. *Pot-Pourri from a Surrey Garden*. Smith, Elder, London.

Estienne, Charles. 1572. *Maison Rustique*. Paris.

Festing, Sally. 1982. *The Story of Lavender*. London Borough of Sutton Libraries and Arts Services, Surrey. (An absolute must for a detailed history of lavender in England, and delightful reading.)

Flück, Hans. 1976. *Medicinal Plants*. Foulsham.

Foley, Daniel J. 1974. *Herbs for Use and for Delight: An Anthology from The Herbalist*. Dover. N.Y. (See particularly 'In Quest of Lavender' by Edna K. Neugebauer.)

Folkard, Richard. 1884. *Plant Lore, Legends and Lyrics*. Low.

Fox, Helen M. 1973. *The Years in My Herb Garden*. Collier Books, N.Y.

Genders, Roy. 1969. *The Cottage Garden and the Old-Fashioned Flowers*. Pelham, London. (Most recent reprint 1985.)

Genders, Roy. 1977. *Scented Flora of the World*. Robert Hale, London.

Genders, Roy. 1980. *The Complete Book of Herbs and Herb Growing*. Ward Lock, London.

Gerard, John. 1633. *Herball*.

Gingins, Lassarez Baron F. de Translated by Barrow, Batchelder and Wellman. 1967. *Natural History of Lavender*. N.Y. Unit of the Herb Society of America, Boston.

Gordon, Lesley. 1984. *A Country Herbal*. Peerage Books, London.

Grieve, Mrs M. 1931. *A Modern Herbal*. Jonathan Cape. Reprinted by Penguin, 1976.

Hall, Dorothy. 1972. *A Book of Herbs*. Angus and Robertson.

Hassell, John. 1817. *Picturesque Rides and Walks*. London.

Hatfield, Audrey Wynne. 1964. *Pleasures of Herbs, The*. Museum Press.

Hemphill, John and Rosemary Hemphill. *Herbs: Their Cultivation and Usage*. Lansdowne Press, Sydney.

Hill, Thomas. 1987. *The Gardener's Labyrinth*. Ed. Richard Mabey. Reprinted from original 1590 edition. Oxford University Press.

Hildegarde, Abbess. 1150–60. *Patrologia Latina* ed. Migne. Vol. 197, from Liber subtilitatum diversarum naturarum creaturarum.

Hindley, Charles. 1884. *A History of the Cries of London Ancient and Modern*. London.

Hyams, Edward. 1987. *English Cottage Gardens*. Penguin.

Kamm, Minnie Watson. 1971. *Old-Time Herbs for Northern Gardens*. Dover, N.Y.

Langham, William. 1579. *The Garden of Health*.

Lawson, William. 1617. *The Country Housewife's Garden*. (Currently available in paperback reprint.)

Leyeb, Mrs C.F. 1937. *Herbal Delights*. Faber and Faber.

Mabey, Richard. 1988. *The Complete New Herball*. Guild Publishing, London.

Markham, Gervaise. 1631. *Way to Get Wealth*.

McDonald, Donald. 1894. *Sweet Scented Flowers and Fragrant Leaves*. Low, London.

McLeod, Judyth A. *The Book of Lavenders*. Wild Woodbine Studio, Bowen Mountain, NSW.

Medici, Marina. 1988. *Good Magic*. Macmillan. London.

Messegué, Maurice. 1975. *Way to Natural Health and Beauty*. George Allen and Unwin.

Neugebauer, Edna. 1960. *Lavender*. The Gerard Society, Falls Village, Conn.

Oxford Dictionary of Nursery Rhymes. 1951.

Palaiseul, Jean. 1977. *The Green Guide to Health.* Barrie and Jenkins, London.

Painter, Gillian, 1978. *The Herb Garden Displayed.* Hodder and Stoughton, Auckland.

Parkinson, John. 1629. *Paradisi in Sole, Paradisus Terrestris, or, A Garden of Pleasant Flowers.* (Available currently in reprint.)

Peplow, Elizabeth. 1982. *The Herb Book.* W.H. Allen, London.

Platt, Sir Hugh. 1609. *Delights for Ladies.* (Available in reprint edition, 1955.)

Polson, Gillian. 1983. *The Living Kitchen.* Benton Ross, Auckland.

Rohde, Eleanor Sinclair. 1931. *The Scented Garden.* The Medici Society, London. Republished Singing Tree Press, Detroit, 1974.

Rohde, Eleanor Sinclair. 1969. *A Garden of Herbs.* Dover, N.Y.

Sanecki, Kay. 1974. *The Complete Book of Herbs.* Macdonald, London.

Sanecki, Kay N. 1981. *The Fragrant Garden.* B.T. Batsford, London.

Scott, James, Ann and Osbert Lancaster. 1979. *The Pleasure Garden.* Penguin, England.

Simmons, Adelma G. 1974. *Herb Gardens of Delight.* Hawthorn Books Inc. N.Y.

Stuart, Malcolm (Ed.) *The Encyclopedia of Herbs and Herbalism.* Orbis, London.

Thomson, William A.R. (Ed.). 1980. *Healing Plants: A Modern Herbal.* Macmillan, London.

Tolley, Emile and Chris Mead. *Herbs.* Sidgwick and Jackson, London. (Possibly the most visually beautiful book available about herbs.)

Turner, William. 1551-68. *A New Herball.*

Tusser, Thomas. 1573. *Five Hundred Points of Good Husbandry.*

Walton, Izaak. 1653. *The Compleat Angler.* (Currently in paperback reprint.)

Wilder, Louise Beebe. 1974. *The Fragrant Garden.* Dover, N.Y.

Williams, Lyle. 1987. *Chamomile Farm.* Hyland House, Melbourne.

Index

Abbess, Hildegard, 15
Allardii lavender, 27, 32, 37, 76
antiseptic properties, 108
Bacon, Francis, 14, 43
Bean, W.J., 15, 25, 30
Beaufort Herbs, 24, 25
Beddington, 57, 59
Bridestowe Estate, 24, 55, 64 *et seq*, 70, **72**, 73
Brunschling, Hieronymus, 70
Caldey Island, 62
Cambridge, 57, 59
Canary Island Lavender, 32, 33
Carshalton, 57, 59
cassidony, 29
Chaucer, 39
Chayton, Miss D.A., 14
Cheam, 57, 59
Chilvers, Linn, 60, 61
Christie, David and Elizabeth, 62
Cistus spp., 37
cloister gardens, 41
cottage garden, 9, 49 *et seq*
cotton lavender, 34, 37, 45, 97
curry plant, 34, 37
Dauphine lavender, 15
Dee Lavender, 62
Denny, C.K., 64 *et seq*
Domesday Book, The, 39, 61
dry potpourri, 85 *et seq*
Earle, Mrs C.W., 81
Elizabethan gardens, 34, 39, 42 *et seq*
enfleurage, 70

English lavender, 10, 14, 15, 38, 76
essence d'aspic, 26
essential oil extraction, 70 *et seq*
Estienne, Charles, 34
Evelyn, John, 10, 105
Ferguson, Evaline, 67
Fernleaf Lavender, 32
fevers, 111
Four Thieves Vinegar, 113
French Lavender, 27, 29, 31, 34, **36**, 37, 67, 76
Gardner, Master Jon, 42
Gaskell, Mrs, 75
Gerard, John, 107
Glastonbury Herbal, 39
Green Lavender, 31, **35-6**
H.M. Queen Elizabeth, 12
H.R.H. Queen Elizabeth II, 12, 75
harvesting, 61, 66
headaches, 111
Hill, Thomas, 48
Hitchin, 57
Honeysuckle Cottage, 68
Hope, Mrs Elaine, 24-5
Hungary Water, 112
Ipswich balls, 91
Italian Lavender, 27, 29, 34, 37
Jagged Lavender, 32
Jekyll, Gertrude, 19, 42, 52
Jersey Lavender Ltd, 27, 29, **53**, 62 *et seq*, 70, **71**
Johnston, Major Lawrence, 21, 25
knot gardens, 43, **46**, 47-8

L. 'Hidcote', 19, 21, 23, 34
Lavandula × allardii, **28**, 32, 37
Lavandula angustifolia, 10, 15 *et seq*, 16, 55-6, 59, 64, 73, 108
L. brunei, 33
L. burmanii, 33
L. burnati, 24
L. canariensis, 32
L. delphinensis, 23, 27
L. dentata, 27-8, 31, 37, 67, 74, 97
L. dentata var. *candicans*, 27, 31
L. feraudi, 24
L. heterophylla, 33
L. hortensis, 24
L. lanata, 16, 26, 38
L. latifolia, 19, 25-6, 55-6, 59, 64, 73-4
L. luisieri, 33
L. multifida, **28**, 32
L. officinalis, 15, 26
L. pedunculata, **28**, 30-1
L. pinnata, 32
L. pinnata var. *buchi*, 32
L. pyrenaica, 15
L. spica, 15, 25, 26
L. spica var. *latifolia*, 25
L. spica-latifolia, 24
L. stoechas, 27, **28**, 29, 31-2, 37-8, 74
L. stoechas var. *pedunculata*, 27, **28**, 30
L. vera, 15, 23
L. viridis, 27, **28**, 31
L. × aurigerana, 24
L. × intermedia, 19, 24
lad's love, 9, 13, 51

Lavandula cv. 'Abrialii' (Abrial, Abrialis), 25
cv. 'Alba', 25, 27
cv. 'Baby Blue', 21
cv. 'Baby White', 21
cv. 'Backhouse Purple', 23
cv. 'Blue Dwarf', 21
cv. 'Bosisto's Variety', 24
cv. 'Bowles Early', 23
cv. 'Bridestowe', 25
cv. 'Carroll', 24
cv. 'Compacta', 21
cv. 'Dutch', 25, 27
cv. 'Dwarf Blue', 21
cv. 'Dwarf White', 21, 23, 52
cv. 'Folgate', 19
cv. 'Fragrans', 65
cv. 'Fring A', 27
cv. 'G4', 27
cv. 'Grappenhall', 25, 27
cv. 'Graves', 23
cv. 'Gray Lady', 23
cv. 'Grey Hedge', 24-5, 27
cv. 'Grosso', 25, 27
cv. 'Gwendolyn Anley', 23
cv. 'Hardy Dwarf', 21
cv. 'Hidcote Blue', 21
cv. 'Hidcote Giant', 25, 27
cv. 'Hidcote Pink', 15
cv. 'Hidcote Purple', 21
cv. 'Hidcote Variety', 21
cv. 'Imperial Gem', 27
cv. 'Irene Doyle', 23
cv. 'Jean Davis', 15
cv. 'Loddon Blue', 23
cv. 'Mailette', 24
cv. 'Maine Epis Tete', 25
cv. 'Middachten', 23
cv. 'Miss Donnington', 23
cv. 'Miss Dunnington', 23
cv. 'Munstead', 19, 34
cv. 'Nana Atropurpurea', 19
cv. 'Nana Compacta', 21
cv. 'Nana I', 27
cv. 'Nana II', 27
cv. 'Nana Rosea', 15
cv. 'Nana', 21
cv. 'New Dwarf Blue', 21
cv. 'No. 9', 27
cv. 'Old English', 25, 34
cv. 'Princess Blue', 27
cv. 'Provencal', 27
cv. 'Provence', 25
cv. 'Rosea', 15, 34, **35**, 52
cv. 'Royal Purple', 27
cv. 'Seal', 24, 27, 34
cv. 'Silver Grey', 25
cv. 'Standard', 25
cv. 'Summerland Supreme', 21
cv. 'Super', 25
cv. 'Twickel Purple', 21
cv. 'Twickes Purple', 21
cv. 'Twickle Purple', 21
cv. 'Two Seasons', 23
cv. 'Waltham', 25
cv. 'Warburton Gem', 24
cv. 'Wilderness', 24
lavandin, 19, 23-4 *et seq*, 27, 55, 73
Lavender antiseptic wash, 111
armchair, 81
aromatic bath, 94
bags, 76, 117
basket, 96, 97
bath bags, 10, 93

bath cream, 92
biscuits, 104
bottles, 96
candles, 99
conserves, 101
cosmetic vinegar, 76-7
cosmetics, 10
cream, 113
dolls, 98
drawer liners, 98
drawer pillows, 76
fans, 100
foot rub, 80
fragrance wreaths, 97
fritters, 102
fruit bowl, 102
furniture polish, 10, 79
handwater, 95
honey, 104
incense, 91
inhalent, 112
insect repellent, 79
jelly, 104
lemon icing, 105
liquid polish, 79
massage oil, 113
mice, 98
moisturising cream, 92-3
moth repellent, 77, 81
mustard, 105
night cream, 80
ointment, 81, 113
oranges, 106
sleep pillow, 112
soap, 91
sweet breath lozenges, 80
sweet water, 77
talcum powder, 80
tea cosy, 99
tisane, 102
tranquility bath, 95
washballs, 92
water, 59, 61, 107, 110
lavender apple jelly, 103
lavender cries, 114 *et seq*
lavender farming, 55
Lavender Lady, The, 67 *et seq*
Lavender Levels, 68
Lavender Lovers, 68
lavender maintenance, 38
lavender propagation, 38
Lawson, William, 14, 47, 51
Leechdom, The, 39
Louis XIV, 10
maceration, 70
magic, 12
mary gardens, 41
mazes, 45
mead, 41, 42
mediaeval gardens, 39 *et seq*
medicinal herbs, 57 *et seq*
Mediterranean gardens, 37, 39
Messrs J. and G. Miller, 57
Mitcham, 56-8 *et seq*, 115, 117
Mitcham Lavender, 27, 32
moist potpourri, 82 *et seq*
Mrs Ewing, 49
Nabowla, 65
Nardus Italica, 26
Ninon de Lenclos beauty bath, 94
Norfolk Lavender Ltd, 27, 60 *et seq*, 62, 70
Normans, 41
oil of aspic, 26

oil of lavender, 110
oil of spike, 12, 73
old-fashioned roses, 41, 42, 45, 51, 57, 109
oleum spicae, 26, 110
palsy drops, 109
Parkinson, John, 10, 23, 75
parterres, 43, 45
Pedunculata Lavender, 30
Perk's Lavender Water, 61 *et seq*
pest control, 66
physic gardens, 59
Pink Lavender, 15, 34, **35**, 52
potpourri, 82 *et seq*
Potter and Moore, 56
Provence, 56
Pterostachys lavenders, 32 *et seq*, 38
Queen Elizabeth I, 10, 75
Queen Henrietta Maria, 10, 91
Queen Victoria, 12, 57, 75
red hartshorn, 109
red lavender lozenges, 110
Rohde, Eleanor Sinclair, 25
Romans, 39, 42, 74
rosemary, 9, 14, 37, 43, 51, 70, 110
Royal Melbourne Botanic Gardens, 33
Sackville-West, Vita, 49
sage, 10, 14, 37, 42, 48, 70
Salvia argentea, 37
Salvia glutinosa, 37
Salvia haematodes, 37
Salvia lavandulifolia, 37
Salvia pratensis, 37
Salvia rutilans, 37
Salvia uliginosa, 37
Scented Geraniums, 37
sedative action, 109
Shab, 38, 55, 59
Shakespeare, 11, 12
sickle cutting, 66-7
snakebite, 109
Spanish Lavender, 29
spica lavenders, 14 *et seq*
spikenard, 12
Sprules, Miss, 12, 57
steam distillation, 70 *et seq*
Stickadove (Steckado) lavender, 29, 30
still room, 10
Sutton, 59
sweet sachets, 76
sweet waters, 10
The Meddegon Myddfai, 42
Thompson, Flora, 49
thyme, 14, 37, 42, 48, 97
tincture of red lavender, 109
Tradescant, 10
True lavender, 26, 38, 108
Tudor gardens, 34, *et seq*, 38
Turner, William, 112
Tusser, Thomas, 47
W.J. Bush and Sons, 57
Waddon, 59
Wallington, 59
Walton, Izaak, 74
washdays, 10, 51, 75, 79
washing balls, 91
weed control, 55, 61
Welsh physicians of Myddfai, 14, 42
White Lavender, 10, 23, 34, **35**, 52
Wilder, Louise Beebe, 14
Woolly Lavender, 26-7, 38
Yardley and Co. Ltd, 12
Yuulong Lavender Farm, 33, **54**, 66 *et seq*,
68